Change ...
...So You Can Change The World!

Our Fabulous Contributing Authors:

Tonya Hofmann, Gene Vasconi, Dianne Bowdary,
Karen Bragg-Matthews, Adil Dalal, Danny Glover,
Naomi J. Hardy, Michael Hofmann, Dr. Pam Horton,
Dr. Karen Jacobson, Sabrina Martinez, Barbara Pender,
Jayne Rios, Kasey Roberts-Smith, Alisa Ugalde,
Eric Upchurch, Makeva Walker, Alicia White

Copyright © 2013 Public Speakers Association

ALL RIGHTS RESERVED. This book contains material protected under International and Federal Copyright Laws and Treaties. Any unauthorized reprint or use of this material is prohibited. No part of this book may be reproduced or transmitted in any form or by any means, electronic or mechanical, including photocopying, recording, or by any information storage and retrieval system without express written permission from the author or publisher.

ISBN 978-0-9708417-3-5

Book design by High Hopes Publishing

High Hopes Publishing

Georgetown, TX

(512) 868-0548

www.highhopespublishing.com

Disclaimer

The information contained in this book is general information for the reader. Please consult your personal advisor before implementing any of the information contained within this book.

Each chapter contains content created solely by the author. The Public Speakers Association, publisher, or anyone included in this book shall have no liability or responsibility to any person or entity with respect to any loss or damage caused or alleged to have been caused directly or indirectly by the information contained in this book.

Table of Contents

About the Public Speakers Association vii
Introduction ix

Chapter 1: Don't Just Speak . . . Make a Difference!
By Tonya Hofmann 11

Chapter 2: Are You Letting Yourself Get In the Way Of Success?
by Dianne Bowdary 19

Chapter 3: Change the Way You Look at Fear
by Karen Bragg-Matthews 27

Chapter 4: A Million Legacies -
Saving Our World, One Positive Legacy at a Time! **by Adil Dalai** 37

Chapter 5: The Difference Makers
by Danny Glover 45

Chapter 6: Rock Your Man's World
by Naomi J. Hardy 55

Chapter 7: Change the World From Your Computer!
by Michael Hofmann 65

Chapter 8: Hunting for Relief
by Pamela Horton, Ph.D. 73

Chapter 9: Two Plates and A Dozen Screws
by Dr. Karen Jacobson 83

Chapter 10: Change the World From the Front of the Room –
No Matter Where in the World You Are **by Sabrina Martinez** 91

Chapter 11: The Global State of Our Social Consciousness
by Barbara Pender.. 99

Chapter 12: Make a Choice for Positive Change
by Jayne Rios 107

Chapter 13: How to Look Like a Sought-After Speaker
by Kasey Smith 115

Chapter 14: Sales Beyond Your Wildest Expectations
by Alisa Ugalde 125

Chapter 15: Unearthed Treasure
by Eric Upchurch... 135

Chapter 16: Using Media to Change Your World
by Eugene Vasconi.. 143

Chapter 17: Make More, Do Less, and Live Richly
by Makeva Walker 153

Chapter 18: Fall In Love with Public Speaking
by Alicia White 161

About the Public Speakers Association

The Public Speakers Association provides exceptional resources for its members. The underlying concept is that people become as successful as those they associate with. This is why the membership is made up of people with a wide variety of skills and experiences and everyone learns from one another.

The Association guides its members in four main areas: Marketing, Networking, Education and Practice. The Association provides those with the desire to be a speaker, access to in-person meetings, educational webinars and a variety of on-line tools. Members learn from and get to know national and international speakers who have achieved their success with the same knowledge provided by the organization.

There are several membership levels of participation and more local chapters are being created across the country. For more information, go to *www.publicspeakersassociation.com*.

Introduction

What a wonderful endeavor!

How many times do you get to do something fun and beneficial all at the same time? Well, it should be every day. When I go to do something new, I have qualifying questions before jumping into it. Does it help a lot of people, does it help others market themselves more, will it generate action and opportunities and when I said "Yes" to all of these I said "Yes" to launch an anthology book of amazing professionals.

I know you will enjoy this book and enjoy reading it over and over to get more and more out of it every time. We are not always ready to absorb information, so I have found that when I read or listen to something more than once I get something new every single time. Enjoy, absorb, grow, and connect so you can move forward!

Remember, don't forget to connect with each author through their social media links, newsletters and absolutely reach out to have a chat. We are all open to getting to know fabulous people like you!

Tonya Hofmann

Founder – Public Speakers Association

Tonya Hofmann is an international speaker, host of the "Change Your World" Radio Show, author of two books: "A Client A Day The Coffee Shop Way!" and "Change Your World", The Coaches' Coach, profit strategist, corporate and entrepreneurial educator, CEO and founder of the Public Speakers Association, winner of the International eWomenNetwork conference 2008 Business Matchmaker of the Year Award, nominated for the upcoming 2014 Global Connector of the Year Award for the Sales Strategy Summit, nominated for the Most Connected Person in Dallas by the Small Business Conference, and nominated for the Austin's Business Journal's Profiles in Power! Her focus has always been to help business professionals become more successful in Sales, Marketing and How to Stand Out from Their Competition!

www.TonyaHofmann.com
www.PublicSpeakersAssociation.com

facebook.com/tonyahofmann
twitter.com/tonyahofmann
linkedin.com/in/tonyahofmann

Bonus Offer: I know that you have lots of questions about the speaking world. There are so many moving parts to help you stand out from everyone else and to make a whole lot of money because you deserve it and because it takes money to help and connect to more people. I know it is my mission to help as many people as possible change their life and keep them away from the fluff that is out there and to help them find the reality of helping a lot of people. I would love for you to get involved in the Public Speakers Association to connect, collaborate, learn, market and grow your business through speaking, so I want to offer a way for you to win a General Speaker's Level Membership with the Public Speakers Association! I run a drawing every month so enter today at www.PublicSpeakersAssociation.com/win! Good luck!

Chapter 1
Don't Just Speak . . . Make a Difference!
By Tonya Hofmann

Too often I find that people don't value themselves and what they can offer the world. The fact is, there is no way that I can possibly live the life you have. You have learned things, experienced things, created and developed things that I just don't have the time, energy or the ability to acquire. So it is up to you to not only give me some insight, but to give me the ability to hire you to teach me or just to do whatever you can to give me the life, health, business or whatever your specialty is. I know that I have spent my lifetime experiencing business, marketing, coaching, and speaking. I have spent over a million dollars on learning about each, testing the information I bought into, developing my own theories and becoming incredibly successful so that I can give you all of this information. Nice ... right? Here are some of the most important personal growth and business development rules I have learned and I suggest you implement!

Rule #1: Get Extremely Uncomfortable
You cannot grow, help more people and change the world without constantly challenging yourself. I hear too often, "But Tonya, I'm not ready." Who is ever ready? I know most of the time I haven't been ready. Most of the time, I wanted to stay at home and watch TV, but I knew that if I didn't push myself, then the TV would be the only thing I would achieve each

night. I didn't want to leave this planet without making a difference. So I wrote down everything I was afraid of on a piece of paper. No matter how silly the fear was, I wrote it down. Then for two years I worked on that list and not once were any of the fears even close to being as bad as I had played it out in my head. So I went from a terrified, silent, shy woman to speaking on huge stages and flying around the world.

Rule #2: Always be Positive
No one wants to buy or be around anyone who is negative. Watch what you say to people. Most of the time, we can't even hear how negative we are. If people avoid you it may be from your tone or the words you choose. Start changing your mindset too. I didn't realize how often I would look negatively at the world. For example, when I would put gas in the car I would complain about the price and how much it was costing me. Now I switched my thinking to "Yippee!" I get to put gas in my car so that means I get to travel and meet new people, create business, make money for my family and help more people. And with this new tank of gas, I get to do it all over again! So what do you need to change? Who do you need to stop hanging around with who is too negative?

Rule #3: Don't be selfish
I know that you probably don't think you walk out each day saying, "I'm going to be super selfish today." However, that is what you are probably doing because you have a fabulous product and/or service and every time you don't tell someone you meet at the coffee shop, grocery store, gym, kid's school or wherever you go today, then you are selfishly keeping them from

knowing. You also are keeping who you are and how truly amazing you are a secret since there is no way for them to know unless you tell them. It is up to you to give people the chance to make the decision to know more or even buy from you.

Rule #4: You Must Sell

If you have a product and/or service to sell, then you are a salesperson. This is a hard fact for so many. There is nothing wrong with selling. You have a product/service that I might want. So, tell me about it and let me decide. Most of the time, I'm just waiting for the person to ask me if I want to purchase. Most people won't just pull out their money until you ask . . . so ask. I can't tell you how many times that I had given all the clues that I wanted the product/service to be presented to me and the person just never asked me for the sale! If the person looks excited about what you are speaking about, then give them the option to say, "Yes or No"! Let them decide ... don't make the decision for them!

Rule #5: Speak to Sell

There is no better way to grow your business and be more productive than to utilize speaking to market and sell. So let's use an example: If you need to meet with 20 potential clients to make 1 sale and if you met 5 people a day, then it would take you one week to meet all 20 people. If, however, you speak at a group where someone else brought together 20 new people for you to speak to, it would only take you one hour to find that perfect new client. So, your two hour coffee or lunch meetings went from 40 hours a week to 1 or 2 hours a week to find the same number of clients. One of the main problems for most people is that they either don't speak to groups or they don't sell from the stage.

Rule #6: Know the Industry

Most of the time, those who want to be a professional speaker, miss out on a lot of revenue. The speaking world has changed drastically since 2011 and most people aren't changing with the times. So let's talk reality. There are 3 ways to be booked to speak:

    1. Be paid a speaker's fee and travel expenses. This is what most people think of when they think of being a speaker. The reality is that, because of people like myself and my other speaker friends, that world is almost gone. I still get some paid gigs but they really are rare.

    2. You pay for everything since it is fantastic marketing for your business! This is the most popular way to get booked. You sell from stage and have a vendor booth at the back of the room. Some events you revenue share with the person putting on the event and it is usually 25%-50% of your sales that you give to the event owner or organization. Sometimes at these events, they are "no-pitch" events so you don't get to sell anything from the stage. These are great for the "after the event follow up plan".

    3. You pay to speak on stage, workshop sessions, panel discussions and coaching tables. People freak out about this way of speaking, but we are talking again about you marketing your business and finding new clients. It all rolls into your marketing budget. It is part of your overall business plan.

Rule #7: Understand Your Options

When you find out about an event looking for speakers or you are offered a speaking opportunity, you have to look at it from a business viewpoint. There are two viewpoints you need to consider:

    1. Does it make sense for your marketing budget? Even if you are being paid, you have to consider the time away from your business as part of the expense. Now saying that, it is rare that I turn down any opportunity since it is part of my marketing strategy to find new clients. But, there are times when it doesn't make sense. For example: The other day there was an event in Vegas that was looking for speakers. They were looking for workshop presenters and were not paying for any expenses. It was for a virtual assistance organization. One of the things you need to find out is your target market which we will be talking about later. Anyone who doesn't want to get out from behind their computer is not a great target market for me since most of my coaching is teaching people strategies that include in-person sales. So going in I knew that if I went, I would not end up with a lot of sales. Now, I could still make a sale that would end up being a huge client but I had already spoken at an online event with the same organization. They were not giving the speakers a vendor booth so I couldn't even work the event. They were not giving the speakers a ticket to the event itself so to meet anyone else was going to be hard. Plus, they said that most workshops had between 25-50 attendees. Now… FYI… except for my own events (and I've been told I'm too honest about my numbers) most events you show up attract half of the amount of attendees that they are promising. So I figured that the maximum would be 25 people. So, when I looked at my budget for going to the event, it just didn't make business sense.

2. The other thing is to look at the PR/Marketing value of an event. I suggested for the same event that I just mentioned, that one of my coaching clients apply. She was trying to show that she speaks at a lot of different types of events -- especially associations!

So either way... Does it make sense? If yes, then apply. If no, then don't. Just because you find an opportunity doesn't mean you take it.

Rule #8: Follow- Up Plan

A lot of events today don't allow you to sell from stage. So a lot of what you do should work after the event. Do you have an opt-in page on your website? Do the attendees have your contact info? Do they have your social media links? Do you have all of their information so you can contact them? Do you know what they are interested in? What I use (which is incredibly effective) are two options that I use together:

1. I have a drawing giveaway and they have to fill out a form to be entered. I give either a free coaching session or something that has to do with my company. That way I eliminate those who just want to win a trip or an Ipad or something that has nothing to do with me. This keeps the people you are following up with as more of your target market since you have already found out that they are interested in you and your business. The forms are easy to fill out and consist of...

    a. Name, email, phone

    b. What did you learn from Tonya's Talk ... (a great place to find out what resonated with them so you know what is working in your presentations)

    c. Comments (a great place to receive testimonials)

d. Circle all that applies...

    I then put a whole row of YES! With a statement

    Example: YES! Sign me up for Tonya's Newsletter

    YES! I want a Free Coaching Session

This is all created on half a sheet of paper that is cut in half lengthwise. They then have to give you the sign-up sheets before the end of the event to be entered into the drawing.

2. Call! You can email but you get very few people who answer your email. The best form of communications is the voice-to-voice conversation. Even more effective at the event itself is to come with a scheduling form that you can fill out right there with ANYONE who seems a little interested in anything!

Tonya Hofmann

Dianne Bowdary is Your Performance Coach for Leadership Excellence. Dianne is a Professional Speaker, Coach, and Workshop Facilitator. She is a certified Six Sigma Green Belt, and a certified Leadership Development Facilitator. Dianne continues to provide servant leadership to Fortune500 companies and to Dianne Bowdary Enterprises.

In her role as Director of the Public Speakers Association in Lake Houston, Texas, Dianne has committed to Changing the World from the front of the room. Dianne has spoken on topics, such as, The Relationship that Keeps on Selling, Connecting to Your Audience, and Speaking Out Loud for the Shy and Introverted.

Dianne is best known for her passion for getting people on the path to success. Dianne has helped hundreds remove hurdles that prevented them from success, and is excited to extend her expertise to you.

Dianne Bowdary is facilitating team coaching to improve your speaking performance. Change the World readers should take advantage of a one-time offer to receive a free 30 minute assessment of a presentation, in addition to a 30 minute coaching session. The combined full hour is valued at $250.00.

Bonus Offer: Declare your readiness for leadership excellence through public speaking today.

Email Dianne with the subject header: I'm Ready for Excellence at Dianne@DianneBowdary.com
DianneBowdary.com
281.608.4876

Chapter 2

Are You Letting Yourself Get In the Way Of Success?

by Dianne Bowdary

I remember when I was so excited to get a new job in Corporate America. I was by far the youngest member of the leadership team, and I was determined to do a great job. I wanted to exhibit leadership excellence.

So there we were; all seated around an oval table that extended into tomorrow. The seats were a stiff black leather and unyielding to the body. Everyone was suited up and seated perfectly upright. As I recollect, there was one Director who was cool, calm, and collected, as though he was oblivious to the seriousness of the meeting. The tension in the air was so thick; you could cut it with a cleaver.

I sat smack dab in the middle of it all. Our task was to share with the team how we would reduce operational costs in our department. We each had a month to prepare a solid plan and then share it with the functional leaders.

Being the perfectionist that I was, I wanted to have an original idea that raised eyebrows. I wanted to save the company hundreds of thousands of dollars. I wanted to realize the savings sooner than anyone could blink. When I think back to the time invested into coming up with the strategy, I may have packed 2 months' worth of time into one. Ultimately, I was very proud of my creative solutions, and I couldn't wait to present them.

The person sitting to my right started to speak, which meant I was up next. All of a sudden, I felt my heart beat so fast I could hardly breathe. I wondered if anyone could hear how loud my heart is beating. The beats were deafening to me. I was terrified and wanted to pass out.

Not knowing what else to do, I jumped up from my rigid chair and managed to blurt out, "Excuse me. I have to use the restroom." There was no need to wait for acknowledgement or approval. I almost tripped over my feet to get away from the table, and out of the conference room. The anxiety was unbearable. I needed the group to move on without me … What were the chances that I would go back in the room, and hear the VP say, "Dianne, I'm sorry, but we ran out of time. You're just going to have to email us your information."

After 10 minutes, I was able to get my breathing pattern down and I slowly went back in the room. Were all eyes focused on the door when I walked in? It felt as though everyone was waiting on me. As soon as I sat down, I heard someone say, "Dianne, you're up."

The largest gulp in the world couldn't take away the cotton dry feeling in my mouth. I felt my chapped lips move, but no sound came out. I kept talking until I heard a voice say, "Speak up. We can't hear you." I replied, "I came up with a plan, but it's not ready. I need to meet with some of you to discuss how my proposed changes would impact each of your functional areas." I heard another say, "That's the whole point of us meeting now. Let's hear it."

I wish I could detail what happened next, but it's all a blur. The embarrassment and shame, however, is as vivid as this day. My physical reaction was unexplained. It appeared from out of the blue sky. I was truly perplexed as to how I could be feeling confident and ready to share at one point and then weak as putty in the next moment.

How would I make it with this job if I couldn't handle this one simple task? After all, the hard work was done and all I had to do was open my mouth and speak. What did this mean for any future promotions? Something had to be done quickly. After all, one can use the excuse of going to the bathroom on a limited number of occasions before setting off a red flag. I started on my quest to research my new unwanted anxiety.

As it turns out, I wasn't alone. According to the April 19th edition of NBCNews.com, 75% of Americans experience glossophobia, the fear of public speaking. There are millions who would rather be in a room with spiders, jump off a cliff, or be lost in the scary wilderness. I don't know that I would rather jump off a cliff, however, I would not have minded the fire alarm going off in subzero temperatures.

Why was it so important to me that I did a better job of managing the anxiety? I was very troubled that in my pursuit to move up the ladder, I would not be able to keep my job. Was this going to happen to me every time I got in front of a group? I was in shock because I didn't have any issues with speaking in front of large groups before. Could this ultimately impact my role in corporate America?

The National Association of Colleges and Employers listed communication skills as the number one trait that employers consider to be most important when hiring an employee. I simply could not afford for this to happen anymore. It was at that point, that I decided to do something about it.

I thought about speakers who I respected and would be a great role model. Our company president was extremely articulate. His words always flowed out of his month like honey. "I want to speak like him," I thought. At the next opportunity, I attempted to do just that. I stood up in the group, pictured myself stepping into my CEO's body, and then projecting as though I was on stage.

That didn't work. In fact, the presentation was a disaster. I felt so uncomfortable about acting like someone that I hardly knew. I didn't know how to be him, and I wasn't even sure that I wanted *my* words to flow like honey. The realization hit me that I didn't know how to be anyone but me.

So back to the drawing board it was. I thought, maybe I could be myself, and this time, I would memorize my presentation verbatim. At least I could be sure that I wouldn't stumble or stutter. When it was time for my next presentation, I was asked if it could be videotaped. "Perfect," I thought. A video would allow me to see progress in motion.

A week later when it was replayed at another meeting, all I could do was shudder. I looked like a frozen robot, reading off a script that was not in front of me. My eyes rolled to the top of my head when I forgot the exact words that I rehearsed. I thought that the words would magically appear and fall out of the ceiling and into my mouth. Rote memory was not the answer either.

Two lessons were clear and so critical. One was to be myself, and the second was to expect to stumble. Who would have ever thought that stumbling would be acceptable? When I practiced these two items together, I received feedback that I came across more human and realistic. I didn't come across phony and rehearsed. Perception is a funny thing. When I saw that the audience was comfortable, I became more comfortable.

The third lesson took some analysis before I could readily understand. I reflected on my first experience with anxiety. I spent countless hours preparing the strategy. I had the plan all figured out. I put together a few slides to outline the main points. How much time did I invest in delivery of the presentation? None. Did I actually need to practice when I already knew my topic inside and out? I tested the theory, and set out to practice my next presentation. I practiced in front of the bathroom mirror. I practiced in the shower. I practiced in front of a video recorder and did multiple takes. I didn't stop there. I practiced in front of friends, family, and my dog. They all had great feedback, and I used whatever I could.

When it was actually time to present again, I was amazed at the difference. Practice may not make you perfect, but it will absolutely make you better.

Six months passed, and it was time to give an assessment of the strategy we laid out before. It was the same stuffy stressed feeling. I repeated self-affirmations. "You'll do a terrific job because you practiced, and you've got it down. No one can do a better job at being you than you. Your family, friends and your dog thought you did an awesome job."

As we all took our seats, I felt it happening all over again; the tightening in my chest, the rapid beating of my heart, and the dryness in my mouth. Why was this happening to me? We had 5 minutes before the meeting officially started. I felt the temperature rise through my entire soul, and suddenly without thought, I rushed to the empty restroom on the third floor. I closed the door behind me and screamed. "Aaaaggghhhhh". It felt good, and I did it again. This time, I stared at myself in the mirror, and I screamed even louder "Aaaaggghhhhh".

"How funny you look," I thought. I tried to scream again, but there was nothing left to come out. I suddenly felt at peace; relaxed, actually. I went back to the conference room, and I felt like a new person. I let out all that untamed energy, and all I could feel was a little flutter in the heart. Sigh. Progress can be so sweet indeed.

It's been years since my original experience, and I've come a long way. I invested in a performance coach, and improved repeatedly with each session.

I was able to learn several techniques, and even tweaked them to techniques that have been lifesaving to this day. Sure, I still get excited, and yes, my heart still flutters. The difference is that now when I open my mouth to speak, everyone can hear and appreciate the message.

In the spirit of changing the world, I am reaching out to each of you who find yourself in this predicament. I'm reaching out to those of you who are tired of being held captive to your anxieties. I'm reaching out to you, who have wonderful dreams and aspirations, and who area ready to overcome and be changed.

Email me at Dianne@DianneBowdary.com, to discuss coaching opportunities that will greatly improve your performance. Together, we'll remove the roadblock, and you can begin to refocus on the excellent leader within you!

Dianne Bowdary

Karen Bragg-Matthews is an author and President of KBM Career Concepts. Karen Bragg-Matthews is an international Life and Career Coach, Speaker and Facilitator. With over 20 years working in Human Resources (HR), she has done everything from managing small companies to leading several HR operations at a Fortune 500 company. She has developed innovative training programs and effectively trained thousands of people. Her dynamic platform style makes her a popular speaker and trainer.

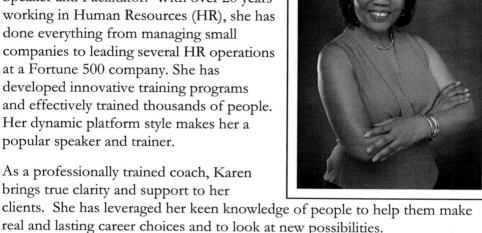

As a professionally trained coach, Karen brings true clarity and support to her clients. She has leveraged her keen knowledge of people to help them make real and lasting career choices and to look at new possibilities.

Karen holds a Bachelor degree in Business Administration, is a Certified Training Manager, and is a graduate of Coach University. She became a Career Coach to help people find careers in which they are happy, excited, and fulfilled.

Bonus Offer:

A 30 minute coaching session with Karen Bragg-Matthews ($200 Value).

The only way to get different results is to do things differently. Through coaching, you are able to create a different and more effective future for yourself. Take advantage of this wonderful opportunity!

Email: karen@KbmCareerConcepts.com   or
For more tools, tips, and resources, sign up for her monthly newsletter at: http://www.KbmCareerConcepts.com and receive "The Work-Life Balance Strategies", tips that will enable you to design a life that is more in sync with your needs.

Chapter 3

Change the Way You Look at Fear

by Karen Bragg-Matthews

There I was sitting in the front seat of the tallest rollercoaster of the amusement park …by myself. The buzzer rang; my friend arrived on the platform too late to sit with me. I looked at the ride's operator and asked if I could get off. He smiled, shook his head and said "no".

As the coaster inched slowly up the track at a 75 degree angle, I began to shake uncontrollably. I was beyond scared. As the coaster hesitated at the top of the highest peak, I looked behind me and I looked in front of me and realized I was coming face to face with one of my biggest fears. It was an 180 foot drop at 70 mph. I leaned back, checked my seat belt, and gripped the bar with all my might. The rollercoaster pushed itself forward and I knew I was going to die. I screamed as hard and as long as I could the whole way down.

At the end of the ride, I felt relieved, I had survived but more importantly, I felt energized, invigorated and ready to ride again. My rollercoaster ride summarized all the basic elements of *overcoming* fear and the 4 truths about fear.

In spite of your greatest desires and best intentions, how many times have you let fear stand in the way of what you wanted to achieve? Before you can change the world or something in your world, you must start by looking inward and begin to change yourself. There are several things you can do to free yourself from the thinking that is holding you back and begin to lead a more productive self-satisfying life. It starts when you learn the four truths about fear.

The definition of fear is an emotional response to impending danger, evil, or pain whether it is real or imagined. What do you fear? No, I'm not talking about the kind of fear that keeps us from walking through a burning building or jumping from an airplane without a parachute. That type of fear is a basic survival mechanism that keeps us alive. Hundreds of thousands of years ago, fear was our body's way of alerting us to possible danger. It gave us the burst of adrenaline we needed to run away from a tiger or lion. Today, most of our threats are not life threatening.

Most of our fears are self-created

What do you fear? Is it fear of change, fear of speaking in front of a group, fear of failure or rejection or maybe it is fear of success. We all have these fears. I'm talking about the kind that is holding you back from your personal growth, happiness, and preventing you from achieving your goals.

The butterflies in your stomach, sweaty palms, shaking knees and heart pounding are signals that you are out of your comfort zone and that you need to be cautious and alert. Here is something else to remember: we have evolved to the stage where just about all of our fears are now self created. We frighten ourselves by fantasizing negative outcomes to any new activity we might pursue or experience. Here is the good news! Because we are the ones doing the fantasizing, we are also the ones who can stop the fear and bring ourselves back into a state of clarity and peace by facing the actual facts rather than giving into our imaginations.

Psychologists like to say that fear means:

> **F**antasized
> **E**xperiences
> **A**ppearing
> **R**eal

To better understand how we bring unfounded fear into our lives, make a list of things you are afraid to do. This is not a list of things that you are afraid of, such, as being afraid of spiders, but things you're afraid to do, such as, being afraid to pick up a spider. For example, I am afraid to:

- Ask my boss for a raise
- Leave this job that I absolutely hate
- Delegate any part of my job to others
- Call on new clients

Now, go back and restate each fear using the format:

I want to _____, and I scare myself by imagining _____

> **Example1**: I want to ask my boss for a raise, and I scare myself by imagining he will say no.

> **Example 2**: I want to leave this job that I absolutely hate, and I scare myself by imagining I will never find another job.

Can you see how you are creating the fear?

As a Career and Life Coach, I work with motivated professionals who are stuck and are ready for a change. The one recurring thing that many of my clients admit is that it is not their lack of ability to accomplish their goals but it is a fear that is holding them back.

There are four truths about fear that I discovered in a book that I read regularly and encourage many of my clients to read. It is called "Feel the Fear and Do It Anyway" by Susan Jeffers, Ph.D.

Here are the four truths about fear:

1. Fear will always be present if we continue to grow and try new things. Most of us wait for the fear to go away before we begin to accomplish our goals. It is like saying, "I'll eat healthier when I start losing weight." We all know it doesn't happen that way. The feeling of fear will always be with us even when we continue to challenge ourselves.

2. The only way to get rid of the fear of doing something is to go out and do it. Taking action is the key to overcome fear. Yes, it does sound counter intuitive, but it really works! Here's my story:

> Public speaking is the number one fear; it even ranks higher than fear of death. As the corporate training manager, I was scheduled to give a 10 minute PowerPoint presentation in a huge room with jumbo screens, in front of 800 sales people including the president, and vice-presidents of the company. To say I was scared was a definite understatement, but I practiced and practiced my speech, and was ready to take my place on stage. Unfortunately, my slides did not

show up on the jumbo screens as I was talking. I had to stop my speech and figure out what happened. I was mortified! What was worse yet, I still had to get back on stage and give the presentation. An unusual calm came over me. I realized the worst had happened and I survived! I had no feeling of fear when I got back on stage.

3. Not only are you going to experience fear when you are in unfamiliar territory, but so is everyone else. Can you recall a time when you were in an unfamiliar situation? Perhaps you moved to a new town or rode a plane for the first time? At first, things were probably very uncomfortable. Soon, you got used to the new situation and you started to feel better. The person who appears confident in a new situation has learned the art of containing their fears…composure.

4. Pushing through the fear is less frightening than living with the underlying fear that comes from being helpless. Death was imminent for Elizabeth Edwards, wife of former Senator John Edwards. She talked about dying, meeting fear and anxiety, and moving forward with peace, love and joy. Right before her death, she continued to champion her favorite causes involving poverty and cancer. In her book, Edwards pondered her legacy for her children and wrote:

> *"I do know that when they're older and telling their own children about their grandmother, they will be able to say that she stood in the storm…and when the wind did not blow her way and it surely has not, she adjusted her sails."*

How are you going to adjust your sails when the winds are not in your favor? How do you move from?

> Anxiety to Action
> Distress to Determination
> Refusal to Realization

There are several initial steps you can take to move away from what is holding you back.

Be honest and identify your fear.

My client Denise, who owns her own business, shared with me that she felt like she was swimming in circles. After some coaching, she realized she was fearful that she would not have enough clients to justify being in business. She didn't want to give up, so she defined attainable goals and strategies. If she had not been honest with herself, she would have never moved forward.

Develop a desire to change.

The work has to start with changing your mindset. No one can make you change. Start with internal preparation. Visualize. Let's go back to our earlier exercise:

> I want to <u>ask my boss for a raise</u>, and I scare myself by imagining <u>he will say no.</u>

Visualize yourself walking into the boss' office confident and prepared with a list of projects that were completed on time or with statistics proving that you have increased revenue for the company.

Continue to visualize a positive outcome to the situations that you fear. Remember, a new path can only be established if it is consistently walked.

Take Action.

Do it. Do something. Some people jump in with both feet understanding that they will be able to move forward. My first roller coaster ride was a perfect example of how I have learned to deal with my fear. I had never ridden a roller coaster before and the reason I was stuck in the front seat was because I hesitated and all the safer seats were taken as I mustered up my courage.

But not everyone is like me and jumping in with both feet is not the best approach for every circumstance. Perhaps you need to acquire additional skills or develop a support system. My client Jan, who hated her job, stayed at her job but started a part time business that enabled her to start thinking that maybe she could leave the security of her day job. She actually picked a date to leave. I am very proud of Jan because she began to let go of her fear. She went from feeling "there is no way I will ever leave this job" to seeing new possibilities.

Practice

Take one risk a day. Each time you take action, you are expanding your comfort zone. At the end of each week look back at all the major steps you've taken. Even if it doesn't work out the way you wanted it to, at least you tried. Take satisfaction that you did not sit back on the side lines.

Celebrate

Give yourself a reward at the end of each week for taking action. The reward does not have to be expensive; it might be something as simple as a chocolate bar, a bottle of wine or a trip to the museum. If it makes you happy, do it.

Allow time to grow and have patience

Some people will do anything to avoid the uncomfortable feeling of fear. If you are one of those people, you run the risk of never getting what you want in life. Most of the good stuff requires some risk. And the nature of a risk is that it doesn't always work out. People do lose their investments, people do forget important meetings, and people do fail.

You can't control the world, but you can control your reaction to fear. By taking risks and saying yes to what is holding you back, you not only reduce your fear but also move forward toward creating what you really want in life.

I want you to think about what you fear. When was the last time you confronted your fear and embraced it, so you could move past it? What do you want to accomplish? How do you want to change the world?

I have decided to live with a degree of fear on a regular basis because I have consciously determined that I want to grow personally and professionally, and I am committed to accomplishing some very ambitious goals and I want to be a positive role model to my children.

I challenge and encourage you to rethink your relationship with fear and live the life you've envisioned for yourself.

> *Do you want to be safe and good, or do you want to take a chance and be great. — Jimmy Johnson, Coach of the Dallas Cowboys*

Karen Bragg-Matthews

Adil F. Dalal, CQE, PMP, LBC, BCC is the CEO of Pinnacle Process Solutions International®, LLC, Chair of the Human Development & Leadership division of ASQ, host of See2B Talk radio, a keynote speaker and an award-winning author. His book, *The 12 Pillars of Project Excellence*™, winner of the 2013 Axiom Awards as one of the best business books globally in the category of Operations Management/Lean/Continuous Improvement. He is also the author of *"A Legacy Driven Life"* and the co-author of *The Lean Handbook,* published by ASQ.

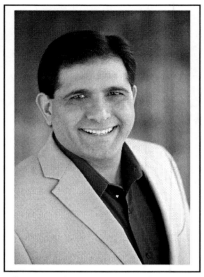

Adil is well known for pioneering several key advances in project leadership and in lean technology. His mission is to focus on enhancing the value of the "appreciating assets" and optimizing the human potential in addition to developing the necessary technical skills for ensuring the long term success of individuals and corporations.

Adil is pursuing his PhD degree in Performance Psychology and holds two masters degrees and numerous certifications.

Adil has initiated the "A Million Legacies" Project as a call to action towards creating positive legacies on the planet to counter the negativity, terrorism and chaos surrounding us all. Everyone has a chance to win a free copy of *A Legacy Driven Life* book as a part of the "Million Legacies" project. Over 100 books will be given away for free to the military and to the civilians who wish to live a legacy and pay-it-forward to inspire others to live a legacy and to change our world.

Bonus Offer: Adil can be reached at *adil@pinnacleprocess.com* or at (512) 289-7080. Please visit *www.pinnacleprocess.com* to learn more about Pinnacle Process Solutions, Intl®, LLC and *www.pinnacleprocess.com/a-million-legacies-project.html* to win a free copy of *A Legacy Driven Life book* for the "Million Legacies" project.

Chapter 4

A Million Legacies

Saving Our World, One Positive Legacy at a Time! by Adil Dalai

(Based on the critically acclaimed book: A Legacy Driven Life: Live a Legacy to Leave a Legacy, by award-winning author Adil F. Dalal, CQE, PMP, LBC, Executive Coach)

According to Mark Twain, "The two most important days in your life are the day you are born and the day you find out why." But, according to Dr. Napoleon Hill, a vast majority of the world population goes through life without finding out 'why' and without identifying a definite chief aim in life. This majority resembles a ship without a rudder, floundering on the ocean, running around in circles and using up energy that never carries them to the shore.[1]

An important fact is that every human being has an amazing potential for success. Most neuroscientists are astonished at the complexity and processing capability of the human brain. Stanford neuroscientist, Stephen Smith, concludes that, "a single human brain has more switches than all the computers and routers and internet connections on earth."[2] Other scientists hypothesize that with a hundred billion neurons and several hundred trillion synaptic connections, the human brain has the capacity to process and exchange several gigabytes of information within milliseconds.[3] The human brain is divided into three distinct parts and includes the cerebrum, cerebellum and the medulla oblongata, or stem that is also called the reptilian brain. Only humans have a highly developed pre-frontal cortex, which is the area near your forehead. It controls our personality, behavior and higher human functions like reasoning and problem solving. Thus, as compared to billions of creatures on this planet, human beings have each been endowed with an amazing, advanced and marvelous "super computer."

It is very critical to ask ourselves the question, "with over 7 billion powerful minds on the planet, why is our world in such chaos, over-flowing with negativity, hatred, violence, wars and terrorism?" The answer to this can be found in the quote by English novelist Lewis Carroll, "If you don't know where you are going, any road will get you there"[4]. With a majority of the world population aimless, yet in possession of powerful minds, is there any surprise at the state of our world today?

Today, even leaders and corporations are simply focused on short-term gains – very few corporations are making a true positive impact on this planet. Overall, the world's leaders have no collective vision for peace, stability and sustained growth – no wonder we can never achieve it! Thus, a common ailment affecting individuals, corporations, nations, and collectively, our planet is the lack of positive, purpose-driven legacy.

If we take time to learn from the chaos and take action to move to the next level, we will survive. If not, it's sayonara, goodbye! So, what is needed today is not merely "changing our world"; but a call to action for "saving our world" and saving human existence itself through collective, radical and sustained action towards a positive change. Unless we are planning a mass-exodus to another planet, we truly need to act as one entity – individuals, corporations, world leaders, celebrities, billionaires, et al.

So what is the primary change which can help save our world? This question can be best answered using an example. Victor Frankl, an Austrian neurologist, psychiatrist and a holocaust survivor, spent four excruciating years in four different Nazi concentration camps. As detailed in his book, Man's Search for Meaning, he witnessed utmost hopelessness, suffering, torture, brutality and death of his own family, friends and colleagues. What kept him and others living in inhuman conditions alive? He writes, "everything can be taken from a man but one thing: the last of the human freedoms — to choose one's attitude in any given set of circumstances, to choose one's own way."[5] After he survived his experience in the Nazi camps, he attempted to identify the one vital aspect which allowed a handful of individuals to survive these horrifying conditions while a majority perished. The answer was that those who were conscious of the responsibility they bore towards other human beings, or to an unfinished work, were never able to throw away their life and surrender to the suffering. Although exposed to the utmost levels of agony, they were able to bear almost any "how" of suffering since they had identified the "why" of their existence. Victor described this philosophy of life as "logo therapy" or therapy through finding meaning in life. From Frankl's example it is clear that, what our mind, body and spirit truly need to survive and thrive, is a positive direction or a legacy. Stephen Covey states, "There are certain things that are fundamental to human fulfillment. The essence of these needs is captured in the phrase 'to live, to love, to learn, to leave a legacy'."[6]

Legacies are what we remember about a person or a country. What a leader, an individual, a corporation or a country accomplishes today, might in the future be regarded important enough to be considered a legacy. A legacy is a concept similar to an inheritance. Inheritance usually refers to material and economical inheritance, while legacy refers to immaterial and cultural inheritance. Leaving behind an inheritance requires one to possess or accumulate something of value to pass on. Similarly, in order to leave a worthy legacy, one must actually undertake worthy actions when one is alive. For example, Abraham Lincoln, Mahatma Gandhi, Martin Luther King Jr., Rosa Parks, Mother Theresa and others have been dead for decades or even centuries but their ideals are still alive as their respective legacy. They could not have left us a legacy if they had not lived a life full of principles and actions worthy of a legacy. Thus, leaving a legacy is not an afterthought or an accident; leaving a legacy requires one to live a legacy driven life. But, it is not necessary to be rich, famous or a celebrity to live a legacy. Lincoln failed several times before he became the President, Gandhi was a simple attorney, Martin Luther King Jr. was a preacher, Rosa Parks a secretary and Mother Teresa a simple nun; but they all managed to live and leave a legacy. Hence, every human life is worthy of a legacy.

So is there any hope to saving our world? The answer is YES.

The key to saving the world today is to create a tipping point of positive legacies on this planet, which will turn back the tide of the negativity, terrorism and planetary chaos to ultimately lead to survival of the human race. Saving the world requires us to use the chaos of today as a ready-made obstacle and a burning platform, which if an individual can play even a small part in helping the world overcome, can be their valuable legacy! Great legacies are not built by sailing the calm seas but by facing the severe storms of life. Corporate leaders can live a legacy by integrating social responsibility, sustainability in their corporate mission and by inspiring their teams to create a legacy for their corporations. National leaders can inspire the population to design a legacy for themselves and collectively for their respective countries. Even "ordinary" individuals can live a legacy driven life. Mother Teresa says, "Not all of us can do great things. But we can do small things with great love."[7] A simple formula one can use to live a legacy driven life is to "LEAD": Leave Everything Appreciated on Departure™." Therefore, our legacy can simply be about leaving our family, our company, our country and our planet slightly appreciated or better than we found it.[8] For the individuals or entities who aspire to live great legacies and overcome obstacles along the way, a step-by-step formula for designing a "gold-standard" legacy using the V-factor® or the power of visualization® has been detailed in the book, A Legacy Driven Life: Live a Legacy to Leave a Legacy."[9]

"A Million Legacies" Project (http://www.pinnacleprocess.com/a-million-legacies-project.html) has been initiated to create a grounds-up movement of individuals wanting to live and leave a legacy. Everyone can get a chance to win a free copy of A Legacy Driven Life book as a part of the "Million Legacies" project. Over 100 books will be given away for free to the military and to the civilians who wish to live a legacy and pay-it-forward to inspire others to live a legacy. The hope is that collectively we can live a legacy of higher purpose and mission as human beings and leave a meaningful legacy for future generations consisting of positive thoughts, positive words and positive actions and do our part to save our world – one legacy at a time".

Adil Dalal

References

[1] Hill.N. (2009).The Magic Ladder to Success. Penguin, NY

[2] Singer E. (2010).Exposing a Galaxy within the Brain.MIT technology Review. Retrieved from http://www.technologyreview.com/view/421743/exposing-a-galaxy-within-the brain/)

[3] Marois, R., & Ivanoff, J. (2005). Capacity limits of information processing in the brain Trends in Cognitive Sciences, 9 (6), 296-305 DOI: 10.1016/j.tics.2005.04.010

[4] Carroll L. (1832-1898). Lewis Carroll Quotes. Retrieved from http://www.brainyquote.com/quotes/quotes/l/lewiscarro165865.html

[5] Frankl V. (1946).Man's Search for Meaning. Beacon Press.

[6] Covey S. (1932-2012). Stephen R. Covey quotes. Retrieved from http://thinkexist.com/quotation/there_are_certain_things_that_are_fundamental_to/346905.html

[7] Teresa M. (1932-2012). Mother Teresa quotes. Retrieved from http://www.goodreads.com/quotes/6946-not-all-of-us-can-do-great-things-but-we

[8] Dalal, A. F. (2011). The 12 Pillars of Project Excellence: A Lean Approach to Improving Project Results. Boca Raton: Taylor & Francis.

[9] Dalal, A. F. (2013).A Legacy Driven Life: Live a Legacy to Leave a Legacy. Pinnacle Process Solutions, Intl®, LLC, TX

Special Note

Mr. Dalal's "The 12 Pillars of Project Excellence" book has been awarded the prestigious Shingo Research and Professional Publication Award.

The World Quality Congress & Awards Committee is scheduled to present him with the "Global Award for Outstanding Contribution to Quality and Leadership" in June 2014 in Mumbai, India.

Danny Glover exists to encourage, empower, and equip others to maximize their potential.

His own journey in personal growth and leadership development began while he was serving nine years in the Army and has continued to develop through his education and experiences in both the ministry and the business world.

From 2000 - 2006, Danny worked for John C. Maxwell's INJOY Group as a Senior Consultant. This involved sales and training for a variety of clients throughout the United States. During those years, he was awarded several leadership awards for excellence and client satisfaction.

In 2006, he launched Glover Consulting Services, and has been speaking, training, and coaching with businesses, universities, and several college/university athletic teams, hospitals, churches and other non-profits. Danny is a certified speaker, trainer, and coach with the *John Maxwell Team* and *Personality Insights Inc.* Danny knows the need for building good relationships, leading through influence, and setting the example for others. He has come to own the phrase, *"everything rises or falls on leadership."*

Bonus Offer: Danny would like to help you get started on your own personal growth journey, or move you on to the next level of your journey by providing you access to a FREE personality test and a FREE 4-part lesson on developing better relationships.

Plus, get a free one topic, 30-minute coaching session.

Contact Danny at DannyG@gloverconsults.com to receive your free personality test, your free relationship course, or to schedule your complimentary coaching session. Use "Book Bonus Offer" in your email topic.

Chapter 5

The Difference Makers

by Danny Glover

Since you are reading this book, I assume you are interested in how you might change your world. You may be asking yourself, *"How do I do that?"* or you may be thinking, *"I can't do that!"* Before you decide to throw in the towel, read on.

I believe change happens one person at a time. I also believe that every person can change, and that every person can be a change agent in another person's life.

We all know there have been cataclysmic events that have changed the world— but only temporarily. The atomic bombs dropped in World War II, the tearing down of the Iron Curtain, the events of September 11, 2001, all of these made the world different for a while, but people always return to their normal.

The world changes as people change, and people change one person at a time. A person's change is usually the result of someone else making a difference in that person's life.

As I look back on my life's journey, I am thankful for a few people who had a place in my life and made a huge difference in my future. These people were involved in making decisions for me or providing opportunities that became pivotal periods in my life.

An Unlikely Beginning

One of the earliest of these occasions was an evening during the winter of 1966. I was a few weeks shy of my eighteenth birthday and still in high school. That evening my parents let me know that one of them would be accompanying me to school the next morning. The principal had called and requested us to be present the next day for a very important meeting. Well, as I thought about that meeting, I was fairly certain that the event was not to give me an award. I was right.

My mother escorted me to the meeting that morning. We arrived and found my principal, Mr. Dent Miller, and other teachers and school board members in the room. That is a lot of attention for one teenage boy.

After some chronicling of my Attendance Deficit Disorder, Mr. Miller informed us that I was being expelled from school – permanently!

Understandably, my mother was very upset and asked Mr. Miller about where I could go, and what I could do. His reply was that I should think about the military. With my mother in tears, we cleaned out my locker and went home.

Two weeks after that meeting, I was walking down Broad Street in my hometown and came upon a sandwich-board sign. On the sign was a picture of Uncle Sam. He had his arm extended, finger pointed, with the caption reading: *"I want you!"* The sign was sitting on the sidewalk in front of the Army Recruiting Office.

You know, sometimes it is just nice to be wanted. I walked into that office and let Uncle Sam have me.

You're in the Army Now

So, in April 1966, I reported to Ft. Jackson, South Carolina to begin my training. I found early on that I really liked the Army. In August of that year, I arrived in Munich, Germany, for my first regular duty assignment. When I checked in, I met First Sergeant Mills who looked over my records and said, *"Glover, you don't have a high school diploma. Starting Monday, your duty station is across the street at the Education Center. You will take a battery of five tests. Pass and you receive a high school equivalency diploma."*

I told him that I didn't think I was prepared for the test.

He said, *"Glover, you go take the test. I have seen your file and I believe you can pass those tests. If you don't, then we will send you to preparation classes. You will get that diploma,"*

Of course, I reported to the Education Center and took the tests. A few weeks later, First Sergeant Mills called me to his office to let me know I had passed with flying colors. He added, *"I knew you could do it."*

A couple of months later I received a large envelope in the mail. Inside was a letter of congratulations from my hometown school board and another document. It was a high school diploma from my high school signed by Mr. Dent L. Miller – my high school principal.

Some months later, First Sergeant Mills promoted me to Specialist Fourth Class, in order to send me to the 24th Infantry Division's Non-Commissioned Officer's Academy in Augsburg, Germany. I completed the training. On graduation day, there in the audience was First Sergeant Mills. Again, he believed in me to a greater degree than I believed in myself.

Another few months passed, First Sergeant Mills called me in to inform me that he was sending me to Oberammergau, Germany, for Nuclear Warfare School. I went and amazingly (at least in my mind) completed the school with passing scores. On graduation day, First Sergeant Mills was in the audience.

Mr. Dent Miller believed I had more potential than I would ever tap if I was allowed to continue on the path of destruction I was on. He made a tough choice and expelled me from school. I had the opportunity years later to thank him for that because it propelled me into a great future. Mr. Miller made a difference.

First Sergeant Mills took a risk in sending me to all the schooling I received early in my Army years. He believed in me a lot more than I believed in myself. He took a risk. He believed. He made a difference.

In fact, the promotions and schooling that First Sergeant Mills provided eventually paved the way for me to return to the States and be selected for Drill Sergeant School. At twenty years of age, this young man who had been expelled from school was now in charge of training a platoon of fifty new Army recruits for combat.

Ordinary People Making an Extraordinary Difference

During my life I have had the privilege of being mentored and befriended by world-class authors and speakers like John C. Maxwell, Zig Ziglar, Les Brown, and Robert Rohm. I am very thankful for the value they have added to my life.

However, in my mind the two men who star in the stories I have shared are the ones responsible for propelling me forward and helping me become who I am today. They are the ones who enabled me to accomplish what I have in my life.

These are common, everyday people – not famous, not even known outside their circles. In other words, Mr. Miller and First Sergeant Mills are like most of us. Yet, they were difference makers.

So, what does it take for you to be a difference maker?

Change Yourself First
To be a difference maker, you must first choose to make a difference inside of yourself. This choice is so important. In fact, it is absolutely true that the toughest leadership assignment you will ever have is leading yourself. Until you can lead yourself, your ability to lead others is severely reduced.

So, let's keep this simple. Here are three abilities that will help you become a difference maker and world changer.

Availability

Being available means that you begin to really be present wherever you are. How many times have you been with someone, listening to that person, talking with him or her, and you realize your mind is somewhere else? You are thinking about yourself, and the next thing on your calendar. That is not being available.

When you are available, you are attentive. You are truly present – mind, body, and soul. When you are attentive you will be more aware and better able to understand the other person's perspective. When that happens you are better able to add value to the person.

Adaptability

Do you realize that change is inevitable? Murphy's Law says that if something can go wrong, it will. Because life never goes quite like we plan, we need to maintain our flexibility. I am amazed how many people I meet who are committed to being inflexible. Without flexibility you will not be able to add value to others and make a difference. So, be adaptable.

In life, we need the ability to read and react. In fact, successful businesses are able to see what changes are needed and capitalize. In dealing with other people, I have to be present in real time, see where the other person is, and then adapt to meet them where they are, if I hope to help them move to where they need to be.

Accountability

Of course, we need to be accountable to those in positions over us. However, we also need to be accountable to those around us and to those we are overseeing. Most importantly, we need to develop accountability for ourselves.

I am amazed at how many people I meet who take no responsibility for their own growth and development. They will attend seminars, workshops, read books, view webcasts on company time and at company expense. Yet, they invest no time, money, or energy in their own growth. They usually blame others or circumstances for their lack of growth.

If you are to come close to maximizing the great potential in you and be able to make a difference in others, you must be accountable.

Making a Difference in Others

Here is some great news. You can make a difference in the lives of others. If you practice these three activities daily, you will become a difference maker:

Encourage Others

That means, we can believe in others when they don't believe in themselves. That is what Mr. Miller and First Sergeant Mills did for me. It took me a few years to really understand and appreciate what they had done for me.

Our belief in the great potential in others often generates their belief in themselves. When they stretch within their potential, they grow and develop.

Empower Others

We empower others when we help them find their own strengths and answers from within. Asking good questions or pointing out strengths in another person are great ways to help them be more aware of the potential they possess. They can then tap into their own unrealized potential and change their future.

Equip Others

A person may have a true desire to change and only need someone to show them how to make the changes. You may possess the skills a person needs, and be able to teach that person. You may need to provide resources or recommendations to help the person receive the skills training they need.

What Will You Choose?

In April 2013, I had a massive heart attack. My heart stopped twice, but the doctor was able to shock me back to life. He placed a stent in the artery called the "widow maker." I have been asked what my thoughts were at the time of the heart attack. The primary thought I had was that I still have work to do. One day someone is going to write one sentence to sum up my life. I want that sentence to be, *"Danny made a difference in the lives of people!"*

How about you? Will you choose to be a difference maker and a world changer?

Use your potential to leave a legacy of changed lives!

Danny Glover

Naomi J. Hardy is a speaker, trainer and consultant on successfully managing change. She is director of the Public Speakers Association, West Energy Corridor, Houston, Texas. A certified life, career & relationship coach, she has over 25 years in human resources and training & development. She has a passion for helping couples, individuals, and small to medium organizations navigate successfully through change.

As a relationship coach, she has helped individuals move out of their comfort zone as they implement techniques to take their relationships to another level.

Her latest project, Rock Your Man's World, addresses and dives into the essence of the make-up of a man (85% sensual/sexual and 15% other). She provides meaningful and powerful tips and techniques that allow you to provide 'variety' to your man through *52 ways to Rock Your Man's World*!

Naomi resides in Houston, Texas and is the proud parent of Joseph L. Dayes, Jr. and the fiancée of Francois Fairbain.

Let me help you take your relationship to the next level!

Bonus Offer:

Sign up for Rock Your Man tips or a complimentary 30 minute relationship coaching session (value $200) by texting 'letsrock' to 22828.

Chapter 6
Rock Your Man's World
by Naomi J. Hardy

Wow! I finally found my purpose. I thought it would tie into my professional background . . . man was I wrong. My purpose was revealed to me as a result of the mess I was trying to hide. You see, my purpose is the result of my personal pain, pleasures and the many, many, people I have listened to, coached, and counseled regarding relationships.

I teach successful women how to experience the *Ultimate Relationship* with their mate. Yes, I teach women to Rock Their Man's World! And I know without a doubt that through my coaching, tips and techniques you, yes, **_You_** can Rock Your Man's World.

You see, I am a relationship coach with a PhD. in Rocking My Man's World. It was not an easy journey. I had to go through some trying times to get to this point. It was definitely an "educational journey." I earned my Bachelor's in . . . "Girl that man is not for you!" (looking for love in someone else's man). I earned my Master's In "Love Doesn't Look Like this!" (doing all the right things . . . to the wrong man). But, it wasn't until I went for my PhD.,until I dove into extensive research, revised my thesis and completed my dissertation that I was able to graduate Magna Cum Laude earning my PhD. in Rocking my Man's World. Do you know what I mean?

So, I am reaching out to you and sharing tips, tools, and techniques from my upcoming book: "52 Ways To Rock Your Man's World…One Week At A Time!" My dream, my hope is that it is the book that every man wants his woman to possess and the journey that every woman wants to take.

What I found out is many of us want to experience that *Ultimate Relationship* but don't know how to get it or what to do with it. We think we can't experience it or provide it because we are too small, too big, not experienced enough, or not culturally prepared. What I know . . . what I really know is:

REGARDLESS OF YOUR AGE, RACE, SIZE, OR LEVEL OF SEXUAL EXPERIENCE – YOU CAN ROCK YOUR MAN'S WORLD.

My journey has taken me through all of the above, not to mention, using the right tools, tips, and techniques on . . . the wrong man! You see, I've been as big as a size 30/32 and as small as a size 12. I've interviewed many and experienced much and I can tell you Rocking Any Man's World is pleasurable and it's HOT. It becomes spicy, it becomes intense and priceless . . . when you apply it to the **_right_** man . . . when you ROCK 'YOUR' MAN'S WORLD. I am talking about the man you have vowed to spend the rest of your life with. So many of us go through relationships and give all we have to the wrong person, and then we move on to other relationships damaged, tired, untrusting and apprehensive by the time we meet "that man." So, we fail to rock his world and instead, we concentrate on maintaining the relationship.

Men want fire, they want variety and they want to be needed -- to feel important. As a coach and author, I am ready to teach you all of that and more . . . but it takes preparation. Yes, you have to **Prepare To Rock**! Your 'Rock' has to be intentional. It is in the preparation that we tear down the walls that separate us from providing and experiencing the *ultimate* mentally and physically. And, until you rock your man's world; until you really rock your man's world . . . you won't fully understand the power of *ultimate*.

A man is a peculiar being . . . we need to understand that the makeup of man 85% sexual and 15% other. As we prepare, we also learn what to do with those metrics. I am talking about . . . beyond the "Pole Dancing" or beyond the strip tease, lies the ability to Rock Your Man's World; the ability to experience the Ultimate.

Now, I know *you can ROCK* and some of you think you are already ROCKING but I guarantee you that there's more and it starts with YOU. Not your man, but YOU. So let's talk about the YOU in "YOU CAN ROCK." In other words . . . let's begin the preparation.

YOU CAN ROCK (The Secrets Revealed):

Y   This is about You and Yours. The first step is to develop a mindset is that you are going to concentrate on You and Yours and not your family, your job, or your pet. I made a commitment to put my man FIRST and it was hard. I shut down e-mail for a weekend – WHAT! My man snores, and I found the good in his snoring--WHAT! Yes, if my man is next to me snoring, I smile because I know so many who do not know where their man is at night and mine is laying right next to me and snoring. Too many women are so busy that their men have lots of time to fill with . . . other things. I want my man and I learned how to keep him and me happy. For instance, I had to learn how to lift him up when he was down when I really wanted to say "shake it off and move on." You see, I made a commitment to put my man first **and he knows it**. What does that look like for you? What does putting your man first mean for you: Closing down the Ipad at night, shutting down e-mail, getting away from FaceBook for awhile in order to not only notice his needs but be the one who supplies them. You and Yours!

O –   There is ONLY ONE. This is powerful stuff. It is not for use on a man you <u>want</u>, but a man you <u>have</u>. A man you want to be with *AND THAT WANTS TO BE WITH YOU* 30 or 40 years from now. This is not for the occasional boyfriend, the "boy toy", or for someone else's man that you may be sharing. Yes, I said it . . . because I've done it. I know the baggage this carries. Remember, there is only one and *he's the one!*

U –   Get ready for unlimited ultimates! Both your man and you will begin to experience "UNLIMITED ULTIMATES" building on each other and driving you closer than you imagined. It will satisfy a hunger for ultimate closeness you never knew existed. You see, Unlimited Ultimates exposes your uniqueness and a level of satisfaction that only the connection between the two of you can bring to EACH OTHER!! This is where you make his tongue hang for you! Need I say more?!!

But . . . There's more! What I've done so far is provide you a snapshot of preparing to rock. Let's continue and see what happens with **CAN ROCK**.

C - Conjure up the Courage to Care. Yes, we have to conjure up the courage to care again. Can you conjure the courage to let down your guard and care? We've been disappointed, hurt, and knocked off our feet when we cared deeply for someone only to find out the feeling was not mutual. These hurts, these past experiences have made it hard for us to care for anyone. It has made it hard for us to let down our guard and allow ourselves to fully feel and fully care. We live inside this wall that we've built where care is allowed to seep through the cracks; never fully exposing itself. Often too scared to care for our loved one fully and openly in our relationship, we hold back and eventually we lose our man or our man loses interest in us . . . and we wonder "What happened?" We've got to conjure up the courage to care for that man.

A – Actively Anticipate. Anticipation is exciting, exhilarating and involves knowing your man from head to toe. Anticipate his touch, his smell, his feel, his look as he gazes into your eyes. Allow your senses to react in anticipation of what's to come. Active Anticipation is one of the most exciting gifts you can give to your man. When your man knows you anticipate excitement from his very touch . . . all I can say is "Wow!'

N – Nurture the Need. There is a strong desire in your man for physical and mental satisfaction. Nurture the need to satisfy the mental and physical needs of your man. Nurture, nurture, nurture that need. Be the solution for your man's pain. Be the solution for his excitement and the solution for his growth. Yes, position yourself to fulfill the need that your man has and does not voice. They don't voice it until they know you are okay with supplying it. Talk about gratitude. That is the best feeling in the world, knowing you're man is grateful for you. Men are like sponges, they can soak up as much nurturing as you can provide. Nurture that need, girl!!

We're almost there -- are you feeling more prepared to rock? Are you understanding how it begins with *you*? You got it, now, on to the **ROCK**.

R – Ravish and Reclaim. Yes, yes, yes!!! Imagine feeling a hunger; a desire for your man. The desire to ravish him, to reclaim what you know is yours and what you know only you can give to your man. Look at him with longing eyes, with a thirst and a hunger that only he can fill. Take him in with every part of you: your eyes, your hands, your body movements, your mouth, your reactions to his touch. Ravish and reclaim.

O – Opportunities for Openness. There will be so many opportunities to be open with your man; to share intimate thoughts with your man; to love your man and experience honesty, directness, and sincerity with your man. Look for those opportunities and approach them with openness. When you can intimately open up to your man and he do the same with you, the sky is the limit!

C – Create and Console. Moments are not given, they are created. You have to look for the moments to create closeness and console what's hurting, what's growing, and what's possible. When you create moments, when you console instead of control, you are well on your way.

K - Knowledge. All of this is knowledge. Knowledge that, when used appropriately and intentionally, becomes the building blocks for Rocking Your Man's World. In other words, the Knowledge to Keep your man.

Now, are you ready to rock? Better yet, are you ready to rock the "right man?" You see, my PhD. is no good if I don't share; if I don't teach, coach, and reveal to my sisters how to "Rock **Your** Man's World!" I also have to share with you what happens when you don't.

I change the world through relationship awareness, preparation and implementation. Yes, I change the world through cultivating relationships; by helping you understand that it starts with you. As a successful relationship coach, I am determined to show you how to move forward and experience the ultimate relationship you were meant to experience. I know that we hide within ourselves the experiences that were brought to us to share. If you made it through, the joy is sharing in order to help someone else. I was guilty of keeping the very thing to myself that I was meant to share with others. But not anymore, and I want to reveal those secrets and share those triumphs with you.

I want to prepare you mentally and physically to Rock Your Man's World because, you get your world rocked by *Rocking Your Man's World!*

I discovered my purpose. Let me help you discover and use yours.

Naomi J. Hardy

Michael Hofmann is an ultimate geek! What is an ultimate geek? It is someone who lives technology and yet can communicate in "real" people language and also has a lifetime of understanding business.

Michael became an entrepreneur when he bought a retail science and nature store at the young age of 26 in Houston, Texas and learned quickly how to not only service but thrive to the point of opening up a second location and bringing in a quarter of a million a year in revenue. The internet and computers were just beginning to take hold and Michael decided to learn on his own, how to program and create a solid web presence.

He also helped a small start-up IT/IS (websites and software development) company go from 800,000 to 10 million dollar a year revenue in two years and through that process grew his skills in that arena. He decided to go into business with his wife, Tonya, in 2005 to help small business owners navigate the vastness of the internet by looking at it as a business development tool.

Bonus Offer: To help you make some great decisions... call Michael with questions. He would love to give you a free coaching session on how to develop a strong website, tweak the one you have or talk about creating a solid new environment that gives you traction and growth options! Go to www.StandOutInYourBusiness.com/ to sign up for a session!

Chapter 7

Change the World From Your Computer!
by Michael Hofmann

This is another reality check. There are a lot of people who don't understand the world of the internet so I'm here to lay it all out for you. You heard Tonya Hofmann speak about utilizing the internet because it is so highly effective, but like anything in business, it is a tool to be utilized to grow your business. It can be incredible for growth and, in today's world, it is a requirement in a lot of ways. Every time I create a website for someone, here is a list of things that I suggest to make an immediate impact!

1. A Smart Website
What do you want your website to do for you and your business? Be strategic so that when you talk to your web designer you have a plan. You can't expect most web designers to give you feedback on what to do and what you should need since they don't do business development. I love that I have the insight so that I can help people through ideas for business growth, but don't expect your nephew to be able to do that. Come in with a plan. Ask yourself each time, "When I do this or someone goes here . . . then what?"

2. A Website that supports business
Is your website just a fancy brochure? Then don't expect it to do anything

but give some insight into your business. Is there a reason for people to look around? Is it easy to contact you? Most websites are incredibly difficult to move around in and figure out. Often the guest can't even figure out how to reach you. Do you have your phone number easily viewable or at all? Some people just want to ask a question so make it easy. Not everyone wants to fill out a form! They want more interaction than that.

3. A Welcoming Website

Does your website make people want to stay and explore or jump off immediately? What kind of environment have you created? Consider the words you choose to bold, the colors you use, the pictures you post. Is it all about you? If the website is your name, sell it with the benefits of booking you to speak, or the benefits of buying your products/services for the end user! So, even when it is about you . . . it isn't. We had a client who sold "High End Investment" properties, yet his website had rotating pictures of his kids with cute captions. It didn't make sense. It wasn't his target market and his concept was too much about what he wanted instead of what potential clients coming to the site needed.

4. Opt-ins

In order to continue the conversation, it is important to get visitors into your social media accounts and your email marketing campaign. Make sure you put an easy click through to your social media accounts with recognizable icons. Don't make them try and guess which icon is Facebook or Twitter because they won't click. As for the Opt-in, why would someone want to opt-in to your newsletter? Most people don't need another newsletter coming into their inbox. Instead, give something away that will excite them . . . something different that no one else is doing! Tonya Hofmann gives away a $1000 coaching program every month to one lucky opt-in account! Stand OUT!

5. Drive Them Back

It is easy to get people to go to your website once to check out you, your company, your products/services once. But, how do you get them to come back? This is the ultimate question. You can't build traffic with one time visitors. There must be something new on your website that is so compelling that it will drive people back. Here are a few ideas:

    a. Blog. Your Blog must be only on your website! Nowhere else. Google decided a while back that a Blog isn't a Blog unless it is at least 450 words long. Google considers it spamming if you have the same Blog on more than one site so make sure your site is the most important one! When posting your blog on social media, in your newsletters or any place, use a "Read More" button so that the reader never gets to read the whole thing unless they click the "Read More" button and finishes reading it on your website! You can then excite them with an advertisement banner next to your blog to offer a discount or an ad for an upcoming event you are offering.

    b. Drawing Giveaways. When I speak at an event, on a radio show, on a teleconference/summit or anytime I have an opportunity, I drive people to my website to get them to enter to win something. That way they fill out a form so that I will know what they are interested in.

    c. Build a Community. Tonya spoke in this book about her program of building a community through a membership club. Google loves back links and when people talk about a website. So, build some type of community where others put your logo and an information link to your website. Give them a reason to click. Create opportunities that excite them to visit and to come back.

    d. Advertisements. When you place ads for a special, a coupon, a drawing or something to entice, not only do new people come to the website but existing clients come back. It is a win-win scenerio. It is all about the interaction between the benefits of coming to your website versus the time and effort not to. Make it compelling!

6. Develop a Sales Process

Do you make it easy for someone to buy from you? Most websites do not. You don't always need a shopping unless you have a lot of products to buy and ship. Can the visitor ask simple questions or do you have a FAQ page? Is it structured in a way that gives lots of features but no benefits which means, are you talking about what your product/service does and how they will use it versus how it will make the buyer feel or what they desire? There are four personality types and it is incredibly helpful to talk to each. They are:

    a. The Go Getter! This person wants to win, they are fast paced, want data but want it simple and usually about how it will make them more money. They don't want fluff and they do want more features.

    b. Social Butterfly! This person wants to have fun!!! They are a people person, want to build relationships, want to buy and feel good about it, want to hear more about the benefits and never the features. They are fast paced and make decisions fast.

      c. Care Givers! This person wants to do everything for everyone else, are slower paced, take a long time to make a decision, if ever, aren't concerned with making money, are into the relationship and always the person who volunteers. 40% of people are caregivers and most of those are women.

      d. Analytical! This person wants all the data broken down into levels of data. They will drive the sales person crazy with the amount of information that they require to make a decision. They are slow in their process but once they make a decision they are incredibly loyal.

7. Assessment:

The best way to figure out which type of personality you are about to sell to is to have them take an assessment or answer some questions. For websites, I develop a strategic assessment that figures out what kind of person is wanting information so I'm not giving too much or too little. If you try and sell the same way to all types, then you frustrate some to whom you simply aren't speaking "their" language!

8. Video/Audio/Copy Sales Pages:

If you have an assessment that figures out what "type" of personality your visitor has, they then can move into another page where the information suits your potential new client. You can then put up a video or audio for those who love to listen or watch or more text for those who love to read.

9. Next Sale Page:

An Easy form is incredibly important. You MUST have a secure page for any information going to you with credit card information on it.

10. "Pretty" website:

What keeps most people from really progressing forward on their website is this notion that their website has to look pretty. It usually boils down to a particular color that they want to use. FYI. Every monitor, phone, tablets, etc. have different settings so there is no consistency in colors from one monitor to another. It matters more what the purpose is for a website than the way it looks. Take a company that makes millions and has the ugliest website out there! What am I talking about? Craigs List! Millions use it every day and it is functional and not image based. Google has only a bar to search on a huge white space website. People will forgive a website that isn't "pretty" but they won't forgive a website that is hard to use, doesn't provide value, or has no reason to come back.

11. Choosing a Website Designer:

People have wasted thousands of dollars because they restart over and over again with a new web designer who doesn't stay in business. Even worse is having someone you know who is doing it for you for free. Some people wonder why they can't even get their website to pull up on the search engines because they created it through a "Free" Tool or did it themselves. Be wise about your business. You have to invest for the site to pay off but invest wisely. Ask lots of questions such as how long they have they been doing web design or what kind of success they have had with clients and themselves. You have every right to get references and talk to people who are their clients. Make wise business decisions so that it makes it easy to grow the type of business you desire to have!

Michael Hofmann

Pamela Horton, Ph.D is a Holistic Health Practitioner

Helping you to reach your full potential physically, emotionally, and spiritually is the goal of her practice. The tools in her bag include her formal education (Bachelor of Science in English and Business Education; Master of Science in Educational Administration, and Ph.D. in Clinical Psychology). Dr. Horton has had extensive experience as a public school teacher and public school administrator. Her experience as a psychologist has encompassed extensive coursework and training in nutrition, homeopathy, Nutritional Response Testing, and Quantum Reflex Analysis and is augmented by her life experience; and curiosity about and interest in people.

The health care system in this country is changing drastically and it is her goal to stay as independent of the intrusiveness of the electronic records requirements, insurance requirements, and general intrusiveness of organizations that want to know about your health. Your privacy is more and more at stake. Your health is your business and your responsibility. She is interested in working with people who value their independence and are willing to take responsibility for their well being.

Bonus Offer: If you are interested in making significant progress rapidly and are willing to invest in yourself, call Dr. Horton for a complimentary 50-minute appointment. Mention the title of her chapter. She can be reached at 888-996-4700 or in the Texas area at 512-931-2162. Dr. Horton looks forward to helping you end your hunt for relief.

Chapter 8

Hunting for Relief

by Pamela Horton, Ph.D.

Jane Doe (obviously, not her real name), an attractive, middle aged woman walked into my office and sat down with a sigh. Her eyes were bright with tears as she exclaimed, "I just don't understand it. I just don't understand why I feel the way I do. There is no reason for me to be crying . . . no reason at all. I have a good job, a good husband, a good life! Why can't I just find some joy in my life?"

Billy Buck (no kin to Jane), bleary-eyed from yet another weekend of binge drinking is beginning to show signs of alcohol "pudge" around the middle as he tells me for the umpteenth time that he really wants to stop drinking and really intends to this time. His wife has said she's finished with all this but for the umpteenth time has forgiven his thoughtless and embarrassing behavior.

Susie Fawn (are you getting the idea . . . not her real name), a young college student, fidgets incessantly as she explains her test anxiety and inability to focus on her classes and school work. No, she doesn't use drugs or alcohol . . . well, she sometimes will drink "a little" on game days with her friends. But that is not every weekend. She's wondering if she needs something to help her focus. Some people have suggested that she has ADD (Attention Deficit Disorder) but she doesn't want to take medications that will "numb her out".

Archer Hunter (watch out Jane, Billy, and Susie), a mid-70's, gray-haired, athletic gentleman cannot sleep due to spasms in his legs, feelings of restlessness, and inability to relax at night. He is an avid tennis player. He's tried all the sleep medications and doesn't like their side effects. His medical doctors are recommending "psychological treatment".

Walker Wounded, is an amalgamation of clients who have suffered serious mental health issues for much of his/her life due to genetics, serious abuse both emotional and physical, and/or PTSD (Post Traumatic Stress Disorder). This person often comes in with a list of medications, has been on and off psychotropic drugs (drugs prescribed for mental health issues), has had combinations of them, and is just sick and tired of the lack of progress toward being able to function as a productive citizen. Often but not always, this person has been on disability for mental health reasons for years.

These and many more have come through my doors over my years of being a clinical psychologist in private practice. My name is Pamela Horton and what I have learned from my clients would fill several volumes. Their courage in the face of some of the most difficult situations imaginable astounds me…and humbles me. It is always my goal to help them get on with their lives in the fastest way possible. Hence, I am always looking for alternatives to "talk therapy" which is certainly effective and has its place but is also one dimensional and time consuming. That is why I have made it my goal to find as many creative and healthy ways as possible to help my clients achieve better mental, physical, and spiritual health. To that end, I have received training in unique therapies which tap into the energy systems of the body and the unconscious mind. Additional training in nutrition, Nutritional Response Testing, and Quantum Reflex Analysis have given me tools which help to support and supplement the mental health therapies which one might expect to find in a psychologist's "toolbag".

Although each of the "clients" mentioned above have different presenting issues, they all share something in common (beside the interesting pseudonyms given them). Every one of these wonderful people suffers from nutritional deficiencies ranging from minor to serious. Research is proving on an almost daily basis that our diets have immediate and long range effects on the way our cells build upon themselves. Cellular health determines organ health; organ health determines system health; system health determines organism health; organism health determines mental health. Everything is connected in this very physical way.

The nutritional component of mental health is one of the easiest ways to begin the process of healing. As a client's nutritional intake is explored, I often find an immediate beginning point to overcoming lethargy, fatigue, and headaches. Guess what it is? **DRINK WATER!** Dehydration is a leading cause of people feeling worn out, cranky, headachy, and just generally "blah". In Chinese Acupuncture Medicine, the kidneys are said to be the "life force". Think about this: the kidneys filter about 2000 gallons of blood a day. The filtering process eliminates waste that the body cannot use. The difference between filtering hydrated blood and dehydrated blood is like the difference between pouring water through a sieve or honey through a sieve. Is it any wonder that someone who is dehydrated feels worn out, cranky, headachy, and tired? The "life force" is sticky and stopped up!

Clients will say, "But I drink lots of tea (coffee, sodas, etc.)!" The problem with each of those is that they dehydrate the body further so that even though you are adding fluid, you are subtracting it almost as fast. Clients will say, "I hate the taste of water!" By drinking filtered water or even water flavored with slices of lemon, green apple, orange or pieces of other fruit, the taste of water can become much more exciting to the taste buds. When clients begin to hydrate with water, they invariably notice a shift in energy levels and feelings of well being. They are astounded. Therapy is off to a good start.

Two more interesting pieces of information about water. Masaru Emoto, a Japanese Doctor of Alternative Medicine, has utilized high speed photography to look at water crystals which have been frozen after being exposed to concentrated thought. It was found that water from clear springs or water exposed to loving words showed brilliant, complex, colorful, symmetric patterns. Polluted water or water exposed to negative thoughts, formed incomplete, asymmetrical patterns with dull colors. You can view his work in his book "The Hidden Messages in Water". Since every cell is composed almost wholly of water, can you see the potential impact of thinking negative thoughts upon the mind, body, and spirit? Can you see the potential for energy exchange from one person to the other from simply the thought process?

Another healing aspect of water is in the research of Shui-yin Lo, Ph.D., a world renown physicist. Dr. Lo is not a medical doctor and did not construct his research based on biological theories. In fact, he was searching for a charged particle that would enhance the performance of combustion engines. In the process, he discovered that by applying tremendous force, water particles would "stick" together forming a "double helix" which not only enhances the performance of combustion engines, it appears to perform in healing ways in the body. In fact, a new kind of water has been engineered which appears to stimulate the body's immune response. It is called Double Helix water. Double Helix helps support the body's natural process of cell repair. It goes beyond just hydrating the body and allows more oxygen to be delivered to the cells. This action may help to remove impurities and enable cells to function at an optimum level. Research is ongoing and looks very promising in treating inflammation, cancer, and other conditions. You can view research and get more information at www.DoubleHelixWater.com. This is one of the many nutritional products that I have available for my clients.

Beyond water, a varied and fresh eating style will provide the rest of the building materials for cells to function at their healthiest. Very often, my clients will be ingesting great quantities of fast food, processed food, convenience food, or single categories of food; i.e., "meat and potatoes" or large quantities of a single food like milk. When this happens, major and minor nutrients are missing and those nutrients contribute to physical and mental well being. Different food categories help to bring about different emotional states. If you want to bring on more grounded and relaxed feelings, eat root vegetables, sweet vegetables, meat, fish, and beans. Want to feel more creative, flexible, and light? Eat leafy greens, wheat, barley, quinoa, fruit, raw food, and chocolate. (Yes! Chocolate! Chocolate is a very good antidepressant . . . temporary, or course). Feeling tense and anxious? Check out your sugar, caffeine, and alcohol intake. Try cutting back. Even the way food is prepared can affect your mood.

Sugar cravings are quite common in those who suffer alcohol addiction or dependence as well as those who suffer mood disorders. There are several strategies for overcoming the addiction to sugar. I will mention two:

> 1) DRINK WATER! Sweet cravings can actually be a sign of dehydration. Before you head for the sugar in sodas (even diet sodas) and other sweets, drink a glass of water and wait a few minutes. Chances are, the craving will cease.

> 2) Eat sweet vegetables and fruit. They provide many nutrients, are sweet, healthy, and tasty. The more of them you eat, the less sugar you will crave.

On top of these physical connections, mental health is also influenced by family of origin and its genetics, parenting, educational experiences, and spiritual practices or lack thereof. Outside the family of origin issues, there are all the experiences that face a person in a lifetime including relationships, illness, loss of loved ones, and various tragedies. All these experiences, especially repeated ones, ones that attack body, mind, and spirit, ones which happen early in life leave chemical and energetic imprints within the person. Treatments for these issues have traditionally been through verbal therapies. While these do have their place, now there are therapies such as Thought Field Therapy and Eye Movement Desensitization Response which allow for a deeper, quicker healing response to take place. My training in both these therapies has helped many clients to receive relief from serious depression, anxiety, and trauma issues which have hindered their enjoyment of life. Additionally, there is excellent research that proves what we think effects not only ourselves but others. An excellent book highlighting research on prayer is "Prayer Is Good Medicine" by Larry Dossey, M.D. Depok Chopra, M.D. also has authored several books concerning mindfulness and meditation.

Sometimes, medication is needed. Most clients want to avoid it, if possible, as do I. However, it is not always possible. When medication becomes necessary, of course, it is important that my client, his/her doctor, and I work together to achieve a good medication fit. It takes time and patience. However, if nutritional aspects have been addressed, and the emotional aspects have been addressed with good psychological techniques, the amount of medication may be lessened.

The theme of this book concerns changing the world. Our world is subjected to constant change, whether we want it or not. We have little control over most of the changes that the world endures or welcomes. We do have control over ourselves. In fact, "ourselves" is all over whom we truly have control. It is important that we exercise good decisions as to what we put into our bodies via our mouths and our thoughts because those decisions affect every aspect of our physical and mental health. Supporting physical and thought health supports mental health. Psychological therapies (and even medications) can then work more effectively. I am convinced, and many spiritual practices teach, that we are all interconnected on an energetic level. Research in prayer, mindfulness, and meditation proves that our thoughts effect not only ourselves but others. It is up to each of us to treat ourselves with love and respect so that the energy of love and respect flows outward. What a changed world it will be if each of us chose love and respect for self and then let that flow out toward others. We will no longer "hunt" for relief; we will BE the relief.

Pamela Horton, Ph.D.

Dr. Karen Jacobson, affectionately known as "Dr. J" has been serving the community since 1992, sharing a message of Health and Healing through a variety of print, radio and television media including 12 News Long Island, 12News WKPNX, Cox 7-AZ, KAZTV and Design Lifestyle Channel. She was the official wellness advisor and one of two coaches for Healthy U TV Show.

She served as a Non-Commissioned Officer in the Israeli Army and held leadership roles in professional organizations, serving the profession for over 12 years as Board Member and District Director of NY Chiropractic Council and Arizona State Representative to the International Chiropractors Association Assembly, integrating business and legislation.

Dr. Jacobson invested years studying leadership, human behavior, communication and the law of attraction. She has received certifications in coaching, NLP-Neuro Linguistic Programming, TimeLine Therapy™ and Hypnotherapy.

In her practice, she focuses on mind-body connection and its effects on health and human potential. The experience of healing herself naturally from systemic lupus has taught her that there are no limits to what we can create. Health and healing come from within, and are dictated by our own personal blueprint: our perception of the world, mindset, emotions and beliefs.

Dr. Jacobson blends intuition with science and offers you the keys to unlock your ultimate potential and live an extraordinary life!

Bonus Offer: Take the first step to unlock your future - Claim your Free E-book at www.drkarenjacobson.com

For booking and programs email info@drkarenspeaks.com or call 480.447.M-I-N-D

Chapter 9

Two Plates and A Dozen Screws

by Dr. Karen Jacobson

The last thing I remember hearing was the sound of shrieking tires, I felt a huge impact and then everything became a blur...

Have you ever had one of "those days"? You know, a day where everything you thought would happen didn't; yet everything that did, was nothing you had imagined and that day had the power to impact the rest of your life?

I had one of "those days" on June 3rd 1998, a quiet Wednesday morning, a beautiful spring day. I woke up at 5:00 am as I usually had done back in those days, put my gym clothes on and headed out for my morning workout. I drove the few miles to the gym and stopped right across from it, ready to turn into the parking lot, when my life changed forever.

As I opened my eyes, I realized my car was hit. The next thing I recalled was someone opening my car door asking if I could hear them. I felt excruciating pain in my right arm, my head was pounding, and I couldn't get the words out of my mouth. I heard sirens and I remember looking at my arm thinking, "It's Wednesday morning, I have a new chiropractic assistant starting today, S*@#t, I broke my arm, how am I going to adjust my patients?"

Have you or someone close to you ever been in a car accident? Do you recall what thoughts crossed your mind at the time? Would it be safe to say that your new employee was not the first thing likely to cross your mind after a head on collision? In all honesty, I can't say that my whole life flashed in front of me, because it didn't. There were no thoughts of friends or loved ones. Instead, everything moved in dramatically slow motion: I saw bright white color all around me, sounds were muffled and it felt like I was in a sound proof room or a tunnel. Most of the events, from the minute I was hit by the truck, being pulled out of my car, the ambulance ride and the first few hours in the emergency room, are all a total blur. If I had to describe the actual impact . . . it was as though I wasn't really there.

I do remember parts of the hospital visit vividly. Have you ever been to a hospital as a patient aside from when you were born? Hospitals are not my favorite place, in fact I was 21 years old when I chose to walk away from "traditional medicine" and healed myself naturally from systemic lupus. I remember saying that the only way I would go to a hospital is if they wheeled me in, and so they did . . .

What personal beliefs in your life would you defend at all costs? What values do you feel are important for you to stand up for? Do you live your life the way you choose rather than what others might say?

The accident had brought up a lot of questions for me and had tested my faith and my conviction. It had been years since I had an aspirin in my body, let alone anything stronger than that. When I got to the emergency room, they decided to give me a shot of Demerol to ease my pain, so they could take some x-rays. Truthfully, aside from feeling groggy, the shot did nothing. When the technician had to reposition my arm on the table, the pain was so excruciating, I felt as though the life was draining out of me and I just about passed out. I was hoping at the time that it would all be over quickly and they would put a cast on my arm for 6 to 8 weeks and I would be fine. Little did I know that what was ahead of me was far from that.

After the x-rays, they made me wait for the orthopedist on call. I was lying on the gurney in the emergency room watching the clock slowly tick, attempting to recall what had just happened to me to no avail. Looking around me at some of the people being wheeled in, I felt grateful that I didn't break my pelvis or my legs or something even worse than that.

Finally by 8:30 am, 3 hours after the accident, I was able to see the orthopedist. He pulled up the x-rays on the view box and said, "It's a clean break." He then approached me and began explaining the surgery. What do you mean surgery? I was just beginning to accept the fact that my bones were broken; something that to this day does not compute for me. After all, as humans, made of flesh and blood, how do we break? I think that was when my whole life flashed in front of me . . .I can't have surgery -- I have people to take care of and a chiropractic practice to run. Will I be able to adjust again? What does my future look like?

Have you ever been in a similar situation, maybe feeling like you are at a cross road in life? Has your future ever looked so uncertain that you had to wonder what would happen to you? Where did you draw your strength to keep on moving forward?

As I am listening to the orthopedist, the next thing that came out of his mouth was the hardware he would be using. He described the plates and screws needed to put my bones back together and the pins in my hand for my broken fingers and of course let's not forget the 3 ½ inch incision he would be making. Did I mention the antibiotics?

That was about the point where I lost it. I could handle the plates and screws, even the incision, though he neglected to tell me there would be two incisions. It was the drugs that literally caused me to panic. Now, I'm sure some of you might be thinking right now, "This chick is crazy; P-L-E-A-S-E give me drugs, so I don't have to feel the pain." That wasn't the case for me.

So what was I going to do? I decided to stand up for what I believed; for what I had known was true for me in my life. To give you the short version of the scene, I told the surgeon, "I don't do drugs" and his response was, "Then I don't do surgery." Mind you, I had a 45 degree angle in the middle of my right forearm, it was far from pretty. This was not a nose job or an elective procedure. The next couple of minutes were like a scene out of a conversation at the flea market. I asked, "Okay, well how many rounds of antibiotics?" The surgeon said "six" I responded "one." He came back with "three and I'll let you leave right after the 3rd round." I reluctantly agreed only to find out later on that all I needed to do was sign a release form and I could have remained drug free. I learned the value of asking the right questions rather than just accepting things blindly.

When I found out the surgery would not take place until the next day, I asked if I could go home and come back. The surgeon looked at me and laughed. I spent the next 36 hours in the hospital waiting for surgery, sneaking in my chiropractic friends to adjust me and taking a bunch of supplements and vitamins to boost my immune system. I had to get permission to ice my arm down, though they were more than willing to give me pain meds the entire time.

What do you think you would do if you were in my shoes? To what lengths would you go to defend your own beliefs? What if you got tested over and over again? Would you still defend your right to live your life on your own terms or would you cave in and please everyone around you?

I was hoping that my flea market scene with the surgeon would be the last time I had to defend my beliefs, yet let's not forget I was in a hospital, in an environment that had a very different belief system then my own. I was the "outsider". Was I going to cave in? No, after all, we all have the right to choose how we want to live our lives, don't we?

Once again, before surgery, I had to deal with the medication issue. This time it was the anesthesiologist who offered me the unique opportunity to have my own self-administering Morphine drip post -op. When I stated I don't take medication, I got an argument from the anesthesiologist who told me I would need it because I would be in a lot of pain. To my surprise, while he was attempting to convince me to agree to the Morphine drip my surgeon intervened and backed me up. I was absolutely shocked!

Can you imagine, someone who originally disagreed with your actions, changing their tune and backing you up? What would that feel like?

After surgery, I had a really long road ahead of me. I spent the next 11 months on disability. Since I had broken my right arm I had to learn how to use it all over again. Have you ever tried washing your hair with one arm or getting dressed with only one hand especially when it's not the dominant one and you feel totally uncoordinated?

I had a lot of time on my hands to think. I was lucky to be alive and I knew I got a second chance, especially after seeing pictures of my car. I had the opportunity to live my life differently, to decide what I really wanted in life and live my life full out. I thought I had done that years before when I healed from Lupus and lived my life on my own terms, yet there was a difference here. Instead of quietly living my life, I had to claim it and stand up for my convictions. I decided that if I had to start all over and build a new practice, it would be in a place where I would enjoy living and that is when I moved to Arizona.

What would you do with your life if you got a second chance? Would you live it differently? What would it take for you to live the life of your dreams right now?

If there is one lesson I learned from my experience that I can share with you, it is to take charge of your future. Why wait until it seems that life might be over to live life fully on your terms and stand up for yourself. What if you were to create a "Life list", a list of the things you want to do that make you feel alive? Doesn't it make sense to go for your dreams rather than live with regrets? That faithful spring day in June 1998 had a huge impact on my life and it literally took getting hit by a U-Haul truck to change my world. Why wait to make your move? Live YOUR life full out right now!

Dr. Karen Jacobson

Sabrina Martinez lives by the words of Einstein when asked, "What is the meaning of life?" Einstein responded without hesitation, "Service to others." International speaker and author, Sabrina Martinez agrees.

A passionate volunteer, she spends countless hours of her "free time" making a difference in the world. Sabrina uses her professional experience in Human Resources and Communications to serve as a leader in the community volunteering in education, the arts and services for the blind.

Whether volunteering, serving on a non-profit board or speaking to a room full of people, Sabrina credits service as the secret to her success.

Are you ready to find your deepest passion but unsure where to start? Start with The Passion Test! You say you weren't very good at tests in school? Well, you'll ace this test! After going through the process, you'll clearly know what your top passions are, and they will begin to come alive and take shape in your life. When that begins to happen you feel energetic, motivated, courageous, and unstoppable!!!

Bonus Offer: If you are interested in learning more or going through The Passion Test, email Sabrina44Martinez@gmail.com or go to www.SabrinaMartinez.com for a complimentary session.

Chapter 10

Change the World From the Front of the Room—No Matter Where In the World You Are

by Sabrina Martinez

10 Tips to Have a Wildly Successful International Speaking Engagement

I have spoken in front of countless groups during my speaking career. My speaking engagements have taken place in classrooms, corporate conference rooms, non-profit organizations, college campuses, hotel ballrooms, auditoriums and, even on, a football field! After all of these locations in front of thousands of people, I was pretty comfortable in the front of the room . . . that was until I was asked to take on my first international speaking engagement.

I was invited to give a keynote presentation almost 9000 miles away from home in Doha, Qatar – that's an 18 hour flight! The closer the date came, the more I thought about backing out. I was scared because I had never been to that part of the world and didn't know what to expect. I was also going alone. The worst part was, I wouldn't be able to blend into the background, I was giving a keynote presentation.

In spite of my fear, everything turned out well in the end, and I learned a few things to improve my next international engagement. So I'm sharing my lessons learned with you, in hopes that you too will have great success wherever in the world you speak.

Tip #1: Verify That the Organization You Are Speaking For Actually Exists

With emails from Nigeria informing me that I've won millions of dollars, I've become quite suspicious when I got an email inviting me to speak, all expenses paid. My fearful fantasies got as wild as the thought that I was being tricked to fly into an unfamiliar country and would be kidnapped and held hostage or sold into the sex trafficking industry when I landed. So I decided to investigate. I began my investigation on the internet. I looked up past events and read reviews. I connected with past speakers on LinkedIn, asked their impression of the conference and advice for success. I connected with the person that invited me to present on LinkedIn and checked out her contacts and recommendations. I called the hotel and verified the dates of the event. I even checked online star ratings of the hotel to make sure that was a reputable location. And after all of that I was finally convinced that the event was real and it was going to happen.

Tip#2: Check Out the Travel Requirements For the Location

First, and foremost, determine if the location is safe. Check to see if your home country government has issued any travel advisories. Reach out to your country's embassy in your destination country and register yourself and the dates you will be in the country. Photocopy or scan your passport. Keep an extra copy in a separate place in your luggage or better yet, email it to yourself so you can print a copy if needed.

Inquire if you will need a visa or if your passport will suffice. And if you do need a visa, how long it will take? Do you have to order it in advance or can you get it when you pass through customs? Will they take a credit card or do you need cash? Can your host get a visa for you so you incur one less expense?

While not a requirement, think about your phone. What are the costs for international roaming? Contact your carrier to see what suggestions they have for saving you money. Sometimes they can send you a new SIM card for the country you are visiting. They can also turn off your roaming to ensure you don't inadvertently rack up unexpected charges. Ask if you are still able to text or use your phone on the WiFi setting to stay in touch.

Tip #3: What Expenses Are Covered?

Does the organization cover your conference fees as well as airfare and hotel? If hotel is covered, is it only for the night before you speak or is it for the entire conference? Can you add an extra hotel day before the event to help you get over your jet lag at the hosts' expense? How about the transport from the airport to hotel and back again? Will they send a car for you or reimburse you for a taxi? Also think about your meals, are all meals included with the conference or do you need to eat on your own? Oh, and fly at least business class for any overnight flights. Not only is this more comfortable, sometimes first and business class get through customs faster than economy.

Tip #4: What Are The Speaking Logistics?

Where will you be on the agenda? Take into account any jetlag issues you might have and, if possible, negotiate for a time when you will be most awake! Will they let you videotape your session or can you get someone to take pictures of you on the stage. Do you need to bring a computer, a memory stick and a "clicker" to advance your slides?

Will the organization provide you with a participant list or do you need to build your own? Can you offer a giveaway to encourage everyone to give you their card for your mailing list?

Tip #5: Preparing For The Future

Of course you will give out your business cards. So, be sure to get everyone else's cards so you can follow-up. Inquire if you can distribute your own survey to participants. Think of some written, audio or video options for obtaining testimonials. What about pictures for your website? Consider a picture in front of the sign for the event or a picture welcoming you to the city, or country. Be sure to get an action shot of you in the front of the room that also shows how large the crowd is. Will the local media be at the event? If not, find out the names of the local papers and send a press release about your visit to the country - who knows, you might find yourself on the cover of the business section.

Tip #6: Phone a Friend

Scour your networks to see if you have any friends or friends of friends that are local. Investigate your Alumni Networks, Facebook or your LinkedIn network for these contacts. However, don't broadcast that you will be traveling if your house will be vacant while you are away. When you locate someone, see if you can meet them while you are in country. Share your itinerary and the location where you will stay. If they don't live far from where you will be speaking, ask if they can pick you up from the airport or attend the conference to take pictures or videotape for you. Ask what other helpful hints they can tell you to ease the stress from your travels.

Tip #7: Safety First

Check your government's website for tourist advisories for your destination country. In the US, the website is the US State Department's *Travel.State.Gov* website.

Also think about hotel safety. If possible, don't take a room on the first floor to avoid the risk of someone breaking into your room through the window or balcony. Additionally when you check in, always get two keys to avoid the appearance that you will be staying alone. Make sure the front desk clerk does not read your room number out loud for others to hear. If a doorman is available to help you with your luggage, take the assistance and check that the locks on your windows are locked before he leaves. If you walk to your room alone, be aware of others that get off the elevator on your floor to ensure no one is following you to your room.

Tip #8: Local Customs and Etiquette

Call the hotel in advance to find out customs on tipping. What are typical tips in local currency for the bellman, housekeepers and the restaurant staff.

Your local friend can also be a great resource for this information. You don't want to either be extravagant or insulting when tipping.

Inquire if taxis take credit cards or if you must have cash. Also, ask the tipping guidelines for taxis - sometimes it's customary to tip per bag, other times, it's customary to tip a percentage of the fare.

What other customs do you need to be aware of? Simply ask when you contact the hotel or Google it. It's better to ask, than not know.

Tip #9: CASH

Always take a little cash in the local currency. Check your local banks and compare exchange rates. Try to avoid getting cash at the airport because exchange rates are highest there. Consider if you need a lot of cash or if you can use a credit card for most purchases.

Tip #10: Things to Bring

First and foremost, bring an electricity converter. I like to bring a power strip and plug that into the converter. Do not bring your expensive blow dryers, curling irons, etc., not because they might get stolen, but because they frequently don't survive the current conversion! Other things to consider are protein bars or other snack food, a sewing kit, standard over the counter medication (medication for constipation, diarrhea, allergy and Tylenol PM for help sleeping). Think about bringing a water bottle with filter, not just for drinking, but also to brush your teeth . . . I tell you this from experience.

Bonus Tip: No Matter Where in the World -- Just Be Yourself

My first international group was 87 people, mostly men and mostly Muslims from 17 different countries. The way they dressed was different than my typical audience, but the way they received the material was the same. Just like every other event, people wanted to speak with me after my speech and share their stories or tell me why they related to what I said. In the case of this event, I was the first woman to take the podium and I was the last speaker before lunch. And yet they were engaged, they participated, they asked questions and, in the end, they applauded. As with all of my sessions, I shared my contact information and connected with people on Twitter, LinkedIn and Facebook. I've also been asked to come back for future speaking events.

So in spite of my initial trepidation, the event was incredibly successful. I learned from my experience and I hope through this chapter that you have too. Not to say I won't be nervous next time I prepare for an international engagement – I will, but I know luck happens for those that are most prepared so I'm working on my preparation. And I hope this information that I've shared will help you be equally as prepared. And if I can ever be of service to you, please don't hesitate to reach out to me.

Sabrina Martinez

Barbara Pender is at the heart of social media. The idea of accessibility is what she takes into each speaking event, partnering it with real world strategy to deliver a presentation that is as engaging and informational as it is inspiring. Her wisdom is as concise as a Tweet, her approach as savvy as a hash-tagged status update, and her tips are easier to follow than your favorite Facebook fan page.

As a certified Social Media Strategist, International Coach, Trainer and Best-Selling Author, Barbara Pender's expertise has been featured on Fox, Blog Talk Radio, and in numerous conferences and events around the world.

You cannot afford to ignore social media, and you may be tempted to think you can't afford to do it all yourself either! But, you're wrong. In fact, I want to get you to a place where you'll say, I can't afford NOT to do my own social media!

FREE! 77 Seconds to Social – Sign up for our email list today to get 7 emails with tips on how to enhance your social media in just 77 seconds per day! TEXT TO JOIN 22828, SocialSage

Bonus Offer: Plus, for reader of this book, contact Barbara for a free report on "For Businesses New to Social Media, What Strategy Make Sense"?

www.facebook.com/barbpender
www.facebook.com/yoursocialsage
www.twitter.com/yoursocialsage
www.linkedin/in/barbarapender
WEBSITE: www.yoursocialsage.com
Coaching program: www.thirtydaystosocial.com

Chapter 11

The Global State of Our Social Consciousness by Barbara Pender

On the evening that I finally had a moment to catch my breath, so that I could contribute greatly to this read; my morning went something like this. It was a lovely Sunday morning and unusually warm for a fall day; enticing enough to not only cook breakfast but exciting enough to call it brunch! So, the catfish was frying, the grits were boiling and my eggs were even cooperating, "how about mimosas"… agreed. I prepared the plates, and this is always the fun part for me because this is when I feel like "Chef BoyarBarbara" . . . lol when I bring them to the table. My hubby came to the table armed with tech toys, and I kindly asked, "may I make a request?" He looked up. "When we decide to eat at the table, can we leave the tech gadgets alone?" He simply smiled and happily agreed.

I wanted to share that story to give you an example of how social media has changed our way of being social and turned it into something no longer special. We can't seem to be without Facebook, twitter and the like. We can't drive without texting or leave the house for a short errand without the phone (some of us take them into our personal lavatory office and bring them into our bedroom). I'm guilty of some of these too.

Can you read this sentence? I b r hr gl hf. If you can, you are moderately geekish and that's okay. Most geeks are proud to be one. But my point is that social media has allowed us to be connected, be reached and relatable to those that we would not have the opportunity to meet otherwise. We now can do more all day with 140 characters and a re-tweet than ten years ago with a chain letter.

What began as an inquiry into our lives has turned into a serious addiction for some of us. My name is "insert name here" and I am social media-holic. I have no 12-step program for you, but I can show you how to turn that addiction into social good.

Here is what is happening to our society. We have increased our communication on the URL and decreased it in IRL (in real life). We have posted our thoughts and content on Facebook, our inquiries on Twitter, our states of mind on LinkedIn and our creative interests on Pinterest. Got six seconds to spare? Well there's Vine. Give me six minutes and I'll give you YouTube. We have become a society where art does not imitate life but life irritates when we don't get that shared, like, re-tweet or tag; and we get too much of it.

When we left the rotary phone era, we should have known that we were in trouble . . .and, yes, that is my generation. In came the touch dial and then the cordless phone. The cordless phone allowed us to move while talking and we entered the world of multitasking. Everything after that had to be better, if not bigger. So while multitasking with the cordless phone, we realized that we could not be without a phone, so we carried them to our car to have them installed. They were big, but they were a status symbol. Everybody wanted one and therefore they became accepted. Fast forward to the smartphone and ,boy, is it ever! What's next? Will we have SOV (slow occupancy vehicles) lanes for drivers using their cell phones. This just in! There is a new product as I am writing this chapter; it is a tech gadget that you place on your car window, and all it takes to talk or text is for you to glance at it. It defeats the purpose of keeping your eyes on the road. Don't text/talk and drive peeps.

While we cannot overlook their progression over the past decades, computers have had the most "morph" in this metamorphic stroll down memory lane. Well, we knew that when we were finally able to get a desktop (or CRT back then) on our desk, that change needed to occur quickly. Mainly, because we lost our desk space! Look at us now: flat screens now replace those desktops, we have entered the IPad /tablet era, and that cell phone got smarter. Move over bracelets and eyeglasses -- we have smart tech gadgets for you too.

So, let's talk about the social good when it comes to social media. What a great tool it is that is now allowing us to stay in contact with family members and plan better reunions. I am asked this question often, "Can I have a personal Facebook page separately from my fan page?", and my reply is that you can try. But why not create a group page for your family instead? Then you can leverage that by going to www.ancestry.com. Everybody can contribute, our youth will learn more about their heritage, and you have another family treasure and the platform to track it.

Now, speaking of our youth -- how are you handling keeping up with the lil' Jones? Before you buy that smartphone or approve access to a social media platform, make sure that you are in control. It is simple. You have parental control, so put the parameters in place before you hand over the goods. You can set alarms on most gadgets to monitor usage and there are security settings on the social media platforms too. You can also collect their smartphones as soon as they walk in from school or at bedtime. These easy techniques will go far to ensuring that you are not a contributor to your child being bullied or allowing them to have closer access to a predator.

How about a positive note on how one kid used social media to get the best result for her fundraiser. Check out this story.

> *Hello fellow MasterMinder's - This is my daughter Julia Ramsey's new video she made for her school fundraiser. It's set to #KanyeWest #Gone. Please head over to YouTube watch, LIKE, Share, comment, etc.! (**Please don't feel pressed to donate**, unless of course, you want to.) What I'd love, love, love is the shares and helping nudge it along! ((Julia is an aspiring actress/comedienne aiming for The Ellen DeGeneres Show!)) http://youtu.be/XyrNeHj5600 (It's a takeoff on the Marnia Shifrin "I quit" video that's going viral here: http://youtu.be/Ew_tdY0V4Zo)*

This kid broke fundraising records at her school, by being creative and utilizing the social media platform YouTube.

Let's continue going down the feel good, do good road of social media. Have you ever heard of Crowd Funding, Kickstarter or Indiegogo? Well, ever need a team of geniuses, money for a project or event? That is what these platforms will allow you to do. Crowd Funding is accessed via an online funding portal and there are different types, such as, equity *crowd funding, crowdcube and seedrs*. The goal is to donate based on your need from a team of experts. One popular example is Kickstarter. I love this site. It allows you to raise funds from your community of connections so, if you meet the goal you reap the rewards and, if not it is not funded. The interest to contribute is high and the projects are normally heartfelt and very creative. A high school classmate of mind posted her interest on Facebook that involved helping her son get funds to participate in his school's trip to Japan (how do you raise funds for that). So, I in-boxed her and told her about the crowd funding platform kickstarter. Oh, and by the way, Mom wants to go too! Kickstarter is for you. Indiegogo is another popular one with similar results. Here are a couple of terms and models to know that will help your user-friendly experience on these "do good" platforms.

The three models are

AoN – All or Nothing. This is when the pledged money is collected when the designated funding goal is reached. If the goal is $5K and you raise $4875, no deal.

KiA – Keep it All. Goal met or not, all funds are collected minus commissions. If the funding goal is not met, it is up to the recipient to refund the money back to the contributors.

Bounty – Any money collected is given to anyone who completes the project.

Notice that with these platforms, there is a huge amount of integrity placed on the character of the recipient. I have placed, as a resource, the URL to find others depending on your specific needs and focus:

http://en.wikipedia.org/wiki/Comparison_of_crowd_funding_services#Money_for_goods.

So go ahead, go for it and "change the world" as you see fit. You now have control to contribute greatly to a family event, a country's catastrophic loss or fulfill a school's dream.

In the next three years, approximately 3 billion people will come online. Are you ready to receive them? Is your business and/or family ready to connect and relate?

Social Media is an introvert's fantasy and an extrovert's addiction. The very best part of what I do as a certified social media strategist, international coach is this: Working with individuals to be more deliberate, strategic and focused when you invest your time on the platforms. I remind my clients that you do have control and to not give it all away. If you need to up your social media game but not sure how to do it profitably, check out my "30 days to social coaching" program at *www.thirtydaystosocial.com*. In one hour a day, for just 30 days, you'll learn to manage your online reputation, strengthen your brand, and become the authority on your subject. Your engagement will increase with your target clientele allowing your passion, knowledge and integrity to show. So, get ready to "change the world".

If you think that you can continue to ignore social media, think again. Once you find your comfort level, remember to find creative ways to be a part of the social good. It's time to get SERIOUS about Social Media!

I'm your Social Sage. Join me to receive sustainable social media tips. Stay Social and until then I'll be right here. Good luck and have fun (I b r hr gl hf).

Barbara Pender

Jayne Rios has 25 years experience in TV and marketing. She is the CEO & Founder of three companies and owns an Intellectual Property eLearning system.

Her first company, KungFuzos Video Marketing, was founded in 2004. Years ahead of the hot new video trend that is sweeping the marketplace, Jayne proved herself a visionary entrepreneur. Jayne was recently nominated as one of three finalists for 2013 Innovative Entrepreneur of the Year by Today's Innovative Woman.

Her eLearning system is her latest innovation and is being sold and broadcast globally through Acts 2 Technology to Christian ministries, and through Express Yourself eLearning to speakers, authors, coaches and corporate trainers.

She is passionate about helping others achieve the success she has earned. Clients leave with actionable items to take with them and execute. Her methods are helping hundreds, if not thousands, achieve success online through video, digital marketing and eLearning.

Jayne is author of "The Interactive Author: Monetize Your Message" and co-author of "Networking to Increase Your Net Worth and The Unsinkable Soul." She is an entrepreneurial spirit with a heart for serving. She is the wife of a prime time, major market TV Director, and the mother of two young boys. She is a cub scout leader, a baseball coach and a life skills coach for teens.

Bonus Offer: Jayne Rios is available for coaching and speaking engagements. Please contact us for a free 30 minute laser focus coaching session at *www.expressyourselfelearning.com/offer* or call 855-456-9876. Also visit our new venture at *www.lovemeansforever.com*.

Chapter 12

Make a Choice for Positive Change

by Jayne Rios

Every choice we make affects the outcome of tomorrow. Every move we make is a result of a choice we make. Choices and outcomes are the result of what we are thinking. What we think is a choice we make. The choices you make today will affect your outcome for tomorrow, good or bad.

We are all given choices in life. We have a choice to continue what we are doing and receive the same results. We have the choice to be defeated, we have the choice to triumph. We have a choice to be grateful, we have a choice to complain. It's the everyday choices we make in life that determine our next steps. Create a vision for yourself and choose to take each day one at a time, making daily, good choices that will impact your life. Make one good decision today that will determine your path for tomorrow.

Wow, I wish I would have known that 20 years ago. It's taken a long time to learn those lessons. But I have learned them as my Grandmother would say, "you've come a long way baby". I could go into detail about my life story and the many sorrows and challenges I had to face as a child, teenager and young adult; suffice it to say it wasn't the best. What hurt me most, looking back, was me and my attitude about what was going around me and, ultimately, the horrible choices I made. My excuse was to escape my issues, instead of reaching out and learning from others and being more open minded to change.

Rosebud

My nickname was Rosebud growing up. My mom called me that almost every day. I use to love it until I was 35 and realized I was just now becoming a blooming rose. Honestly, I really should have been a blooming rose in my 20's. But here I am in my mid 30's and just realizing my full potential and what I was intended to be; a loving, caring, thoughtful person with strength, dignity and a bright future in front of me. How the choices I made in life would have been so much better ,if I had only known this before.

You see a Rosebud is beautiful, but it's closed. It hides inside itself for protection and shelter, it's comfortable in there. Its petals are not exposed, so not to get withered by the storm. It doesn't and can't reach out to anyone for help because it doesn't know how to open and be exposed. Trust is a very difficult thing to do for the Rosebud. If it doesn't open, it thinks it is safe.

The truth is the Rosebud wants to open because that is what it was made to do, but it doesn't know which petal to open first. If it exposes one petal, will it need to expose them all? Will there be other roses out there like it? Can it protect itself from the storm if exposed?

These are a lot of issues I related to as the Rosebud. My head told me that no one was going through or went through what I did. I saw one crowd and thought, "I am not as good as they are; they won't understand me". I saw my girlfriends had really great family lives and I could see the difference and always compared my life to theirs. Of course, they loved me for me, but not until I was a Blooming Rose did I realize that. I felt less than other people, it was a bad feeling. And, of course, my head played along, I would stop myself before I started, I would second guess myself in everything I did, I let others opinions sway me left then right, I was a people pleaser always looking out for the other person but neglecting myself. This went on for over 20 years. Needless to say, the choices I was making were not of sound mind.

The other day a friend and I were talking, she knows I am writing about Choices in Life, and we were talking about a situation I was in, resulting from a choice I made 17 years ago and she said, well it's the choice you made. I told her, yes, but that choice was a result of my environment, not being of sound mind, and not being capable of making "good, positive" choices for myself. So, now I had the choice to end it or make the best of it. I was choosing to turn it around and make the best of it . . . but I still have a choice. No matter what age, you have a choice.

The Rosebud must take it day by day, moment by moment. Each petal must open and begin feeling its worth. Day by day, it makes the choice to get up, move and open itself to the elements of this world. Each day it gets more strength to open more petals and trust more. Every new element is a precious gift and valuable lesson. Raindrops become its best friend . . . in those storms it learns its greatest lessons and receives more strength. In the sunshine it learns to feel joy, love, peace and hope. It strives each day to become a fully developed Blooming Rose.

Blooming Rose

A Blooming Rose, which I proudly call myself today, is open and free and feels beautiful on the inside and is not afraid to show it off. It's open to the outside air, sunshine and all of the weather elements. Its learned that nobody's life is perfect and it's okay to make mistakes. It's open and honest about its life and every petal is a precious trophy. Every petal is unique and with every rain drop is a valuable lesson. The Blooming Rose knows its value and realizes every day is a precious moment, so it enjoys itself; dancing in the wind and sending out sweet fragrance for all who come near.
What I have learned working with my clients is that no matter your age, you can become a Blooming Rose. It starts with believing in yourself, connecting with the right people, and learning the secret to turning off negativity in your head and switching it with positive thoughts. Blooming Rose's know the power within themselves and aren't afraid to show it and share it.

Skip Ahead, I am 45 -- a Full Blown Rose

The past 10 years living as a full blown rose have been incredible! I have many friends, I have built 3 companies, I have 2 great kids I get to spend every day with, a fabulous husband and I could go on (but for time sake I will stop:-). I have allowed myself to be free and to love and to let people in. So many new opportunities have opened up for me and it continues to this day. The choices I make daily are in sound mind and I allow myself to say no and feel fine about it (that's a great feeling in itself, try it). I choose to wake up thankful. I choose to go to bed thankful. Being grateful for what you have is a big step in feeling good about your life. When I was in Africa videotaping an eLearning course, I realized VERY quickly how lucky and blessed we are in the United States. When kids are walking down the street with no shoes on their feet and mom's crying because their babies are dying from malaria and no one can do anything . . . it's time to look in the mirror and make a choice. Complain or be Grateful. Make a good choice each day, choose to be positive and watch the difference it will make in your life.

It took me 20 years to learn this lesson and here's how I went from Rosebud to Blooming Rose.

1. I located really good books that came highly recommended by friends and associates (Breaking Free by Beth Moore is excellent) (I never did the counselor route, but for some, this is a really good option, find a Christian Counselor.)
2. I forgave everyone who I thought had hurt me, intentionally or not.
3. I wrote down the goals I wanted for MY life (not based on past, current environment or whatever else . . . this is what I wanted for my life). The dream I had as a child, or the new dreams I had for a better future.
4. Given my current situation, I wrote down the steps it would take and the choices I would have to make to have that life and achieve MY dreams. (I say given situation because you may have to get up and MOVE to get out from where you are to achieve the life YOU want. This is sometimes easier said than done.) But, if you are in a situation you KNOW is not right for you,

please start an action plan to move forward and make the right choice for YOU, not anyone else. Only YOU know what's best for YOU and until now you may not have realized that YOU have a CHOICE.

5. I began to visualize myself living that dream life and every day I made small choices that moved me closer to my goals and dreams.

6. I began reading the Bible about who God says I am and that was powerful!

7. I stopped listening to the negative thoughts in my head. Some people put rubber bands around their wrists and when they begin thinking a negative thought they pop themselves, I am not suggesting this...but whatever works! It took almost one whole year for me to finally master this. Now when I get bad thoughts I am quick to respond and switch my thought process to positive thoughts. This is an important step to self doubt. Only you can master your thoughts. Ask God for help, read the Word, it's full of positive reinforcement and will remind you of who you really are!

8. I started to realize how grateful I was for everything in life. My trip to Africa was life changing. If you are bitter or jealous or think life is unfair, take a trip to a third world country and you will begin to count your MANY blessings. Now every day I wake up and the first two words out of my mouth are Thank you and I truly mean it. I start a running list in my head of all of the things I am thankful for and before you know it I have talked myself into a pretty good mood!

9. PRACTICE, PRACTICE, PRACTICE. These steps take practice, but before you know it, it's automatic. If you think negative thoughts, practice replacing them with positive thoughts. If you need direction, practice writing goals and dreams. After you write your action plan, practice choosing one

step per day toward your dream. If you are shy and closed in your environment, practice putting yourself out there at a networking event. It's one daily choice at a time

Conclusion

The choices we make every day affect our life tomorrow, 10 days from now and even 10 years from now. Make a choice for positive change today and change your world for the better!

Jayne Rios

Kasey Smith, Image Consultant and Color Specialist, has a background in fashion merchandising, double degrees in fashion design and pattern drafting, and is the past owner of a costume rental and design company. When she added image consulting to the mix she had an epiphany: Fashion is about Clothing . . . Image is about People!

For Kasey, the work is about helping each person connect with her true essence and then communicate that message through her Appearance, Behavior, and Communication . . . the ABCs of Image. Kasey is a graduate of London Image Institute, Appearance Design Institute, and Sci-Art Global. She is a member of the Association of Image Consultants International (AICI) and Colour Designers International (CDI). She is a certified mentor through Women of Visionary Influence (WOVI). Kasey is a professional speaker, trainer, and workshop facilitator and is a member of Toastmasters International, Speaker Co-op of Dallas, National Speakers Association, National Speakers Association North Texas, and Public Speakers Association.

Her company is Artistry of Image. Kasey believes we are all living works of art . . . masterpieces, actually . . . some of us just need a little tweaking!

Bonus Offer: To get started on your journey to Look Like a Sought-After Speaker, download your two free reports, Color Psychology 2.0 and Wardrobe Building Template, at www.artistryofimage.com/llasas.
214-837-1814
kasey@artistryofimage.com
www.artistryofimage.com

Chapter 13

How to Look Like a Sought-After Speaker

by Kasey Smith

Imagine . . . you're about to walk on stage. The room is full of potential clients and referrals. Your content is ready—full of great stories to illustrate your points. Your ideas are fresh and innovative. Your solutions will make a difference for your audience.

You want to make a great first impression, so they will see you as credible, reliable, and trustworthy. However, before you say a word, your Appearance, Behavior, and non-verbal Communication are transmitting messages about you whether you are aware of them or not. This triad is the ABCs of Image. All three are integrated into your image, because all three are expressed as you interact with people. These visual messages can interfere with your success, if they do not represent the real you.

As human beings, we are walking billboards, transmitting information about ourselves that is subconsciously picked up by others. We are hard-wired to make snap judgments about our environment. This has to do with our fight, flight, or freeze responses. It's a subconscious mechanism that is supposed to keep us safe, out of harm's way. Even when we are safe—no real or metaphorical lions, tigers, or bears chasing us—this built-into-our-genes assessment tool kicks in, and we judge everything around us.

This is why first impressions are made in ten seconds or less. It doesn't seem fair, does it? It's just the way we're wired. We are all connected. We are all intuitive. We sense when someone is being genuine, if their message is congruent and believable.

From the stage, these messages are picked up by the audience. They don't know how they know or why they know—they just intuitively know. The unconscious question becomes, "Are you a friend who can be trusted or a foe to keep at arm's length?"

Authenticity is the key to being likeable onstage and off. Being authentic requires getting clear on who you are on the INSIDE—your essence—then visually and auditorily communicating that message on the OUTSIDE—your presence. Socrates said it best: "Know thyself."

The more you define your core essence and express yourself authentically, the more connected you are to yourself and others. You are more relatable, congruent, and memorable. You are heard more effectively and seen as credible, reliable, and trustworthy.

The following strategies will be helpful in determining your speaker wardrobe—the key to looking like a sought-after speaker. You can immediately apply these strategies to what's in your closet now, and you can also begin building a wardrobe that is so comprehensive you can have an outfit for every occasion.

First Impressions

Your appearance is what people notice first. From a distance, color and silhouette are the first things they see—essentially, your clothes. As they get closer and closer, you want them to notice you, who you are, your confidence, your authenticity, your professional presence. If up close, your clothes are STILL all they see, then your clothes are wearing you, rather than complimenting you.

Problems arise when you wear colors, design lines, and wardrobe pieces that are not in harmony with you. Being in alignment with your clothing is like tuning in to the right radio frequency or connecting to the right URL address. When your frequency is in alignment with your clothing—details that are a match to you—you are connected. You look radiant, alive, attractive, and real.

Your Image Is Showing 24/7

Your presentation starts long before you walk on stage. You must keep in mind the potential to be seen by meeting planners or participants before or after you speak. Your reputation and credibility are at stake if you appear to be unprofessional in any way, whether verbal or non-verbal.

We have all seen tempers flare or inappropriate behavior at the ticket counter, baggage claim, or hotel check-in. Can you imagine, in any of these situations, seeing that person on the agenda as your next presenter? His or her credibility would be lost before even walking onto the stage.

Have strategies set up for before and after speaking so you don't fall victim to last-minute details. Give yourself enough time to check in with the meeting planner and mingle with the participants. By creating rapport with them before your speech, you'll have a warmed-up and receptive audience.

Be Aware of Distractions

Make sure your clothes are appropriate for the audience and venue and still be yourself. Women: do not wear clothes that are too tight, too shiny, clingy, or low-cut. Men: wear a suit if it is part of your business wardrobe; don't wear one because you think is it what a speaker is "supposed to look like."

Be aware of noisy or shiny jewelry. The light may reflect back on the audience, and the noise will certainly be distracting, especially if you are wearing a mike.

Be aware of your behavior. Do you have any subconscious, repetitive gestures that need to be eliminated? Or filler words or phrases that are distracting? Work on eliminating them.

Your communication is as much non-verbal as it is verbal, if not more. How's your posture? Are you smiling? Should you be smiling? Consider how you relate to your audience through your stance, movement, gestures, eye contact, and facial expressions.

What to Wear for Your Video

Solid colors work best—not too light, too dark, or too bright. Be aware of the backdrop, and don't blend in to it by wearing similar colors. Patterns (stripes, paisley, herringbone, tweed, etc.) create a blurred, moiré effect that appears to vibrate on camera.

Avoid distracting jewelry or other accessories and reflective or shiny fabric, as the microphone picks up noise, and the camera catches the light from shiny surfaces. Wear a jacket or top that can accommodate a lapel mike. Take an extra outfit or two—just in case!

Color Psychology

Color is refracted light. Each color has its own wavelength and vibrates at its own distinct frequency. Each frequency connects us to an emotional response. When we see red, yellow, or green . . . we feel passion, joy, or calm. Keep the psychology of color in mind as you think about what colors to wear. What response are you after?

Black is the ultimate power color, yet many people don't look good in black. It is important to find out what your power color is. Or, if you are wearing black as a neutral, finding out if there is a better formal neutral for you would be valuable.

Blue is the color to wear when you want to be approachable or show sincerity, truth, loyalty, and friendliness. The question is—what intensity of blue is right for you?

Yellow is the color the eye sees first. Wear it to be noticed or increase concentration in your audience. Too much, though, can increase anxiety. Again, the question is—do you look good in yellow and if yes, what color of yellow is your yellow?

Your Color

Having your color palette done is a great investment because it reveals your very best colors. These include your personal colors, neutrals, reds and dramatics—including your power color, subdued colors, pastels, prints, patterns, and metals.

Wearing your best colors will make you look younger, thinner, and healthy. Wearing colors that are wrong for you will make you look older, heavier, and sickly.

Begin wearing your personal colors—your hair, eyes, skin-tone, and your best "white." Avoid wearing a white that is whiter than your teeth or the whites of your eyes; it will make your teeth appear more on the yellow side, your eyes won't look as bright, and it could wash you out, especially if it is stark white.

Your Style

Your style is the manner in which you put your clothing and accessories together. It is your story expressed visually through the clothes you choose to wear and how you choose to wear them.

Having style is being comfortable in your clothes and being confident in your selections. It is knowing what is right for you and what is not right for you. It is also having the conviction to buy only what works on your body, regardless of trends.

Having style is not about spending huge amounts of money. It's about being creative—mixing items together that interest you and make you interesting and unique. It is about creating your Signature Look.

Your Fit

Your clothes need to fit you properly. They should hang straight from your shoulder line and skim the outline of your body with no pulling, puckering, gapping, or bagging.

Alterations are a must when a garment does not fit correctly. Men typically know they have to tailor their clothes. Women tend to think clothes should fit right off the rack—and when they don't fit, they think something is wrong with them, not the clothes. It is not you. All brands have different sizing and fit specifications.

Find a good tailor or seamstress and get familiar with what that person can do for you. Then, when you find an item you love, you will know if it can be altered or not. It's the finer attention to detail that makes the difference in looking put together or thrown together.

Your Wardrobe

It's important to have a budget for clothing, accessories, grooming, and hair/nail care. Choose investment clothing with classic styling that will potentially last five years or more. It is better to have fewer pieces with better quality materials.

Think capsule dressing—eight to twelve pieces that mix and match, creating several different outfits, several different looks. Each capsule has a color theme: a neutral, a dramatic, and a print. It is built with five core pieces. Women: jackets, tops, pants, skirts, dresses. Men: jackets, shirts, pants, ties, jeans.

Accessories set the tone for each combination and can cross over to other capsules for more options. Start by identifying items you already have that a capsule can be built upon.

Cost-Per-Wear Formula

Looking at the cost-per-wear formula will give you a clearer picture of the value of choosing better quality investment clothing for your speaker wardrobe.

Cost-per-wear formula: Divide cost of item by number of outfits you can wear it with.

Example: $300 jacket worn with two skirts, two pants, and a dress becomes a $60 jacket (300/5).

Worn 30 times per year, cost per wearing is just $2. If worn for five years—it is now a 40-cent jacket (2/5). Calculate the cost of each garment with tailoring included.

Power Piece in Your Closet

A jacket or sweater, called "the third piece," speaks of authority. For example, a doctor's third piece is his or her lab coat.

Traditionally, women have worn jackets on the platform because it gives them perceived authority. However, a new trend is emerging. Some speakers are going for a less formal look, going sleeveless, even wearing cocktail attire on stage.

My advice—don't listen to the trends or to tradition—listen inside yourself. Discover your authentic self and create a style of dressing that communicates who you are—authentically.

Authenticity

Looking like a sought-after speaker is all about being authentic. Authenticity comes with knowing yourself inside and out. It's time to get clear, confident, and comfortable in your wardrobe choices. The result: you can be "in the moment" with your audience—without wardrobe distractions—masterfully delivering your message.

Kasey Smith

Alisa Ugalde is an expert in the domain of sales—she laser pinpoints precisely where *you* are falling short and shows you how to burst through *your* sales challenges so that your business flips from potential to profit.

You are an expert in your business. For you there's not a lot of distinction between what you love, what you're good at, and what you do for a living. You are brilliant when it comes to satisfying your clients— you're just not landing them! And you are frustrated. You know something needs to change in your business. You're not making enough money... even though you seem to be working hard and giving it your all. But you LOVE what you do. You absolutely love your business.

As a Certified School Teacher, Alisa began her career as the top-producing sales person in the Country for 3 different sales organizations. Her consistent track record of regularly outperforming her fellow sales reps nationwide, earned her a reputation of success that follows her to this day.

Alisa serves the needs of mission-driven entrepreneurs, whose businesses depend on sales, by helping self-employed women solve one of their biggest business problems: How do I get clients to say yes? Wondering how? Go to www.ClaimClients.com for your free checklist to get started.

Bonus Offer: Set up a no cost Sales Breakthrough with Alisa Ugalde TODAY at ClaimYourClients.com

Chapter 14

Sales Beyond Your Wildest Expectations

by Alisa Ugalde

3 Secrets to Stop Potential Sales from Slip Sliding Away

Looking to Change Your World and get paid? You're About to Discover Exactly How to Exponentially Increase Your Sales with Comfort and Ease Without all the Pushing and Pressure that Everyone Hates, so You Can Deliver Your Expertise and choose whether you want to save, donate or spend your income!

To prevent buyers from procrastinating, consider 1) Being extremely specific when describing your solution, 2) Lead the prospect through the effects, consequences and cost of staying in their current situation, and 3) Convey what their new world would be like after working with you.

I was talking to my client, Carla, and it became clear to me that she didn't start her business because she wanted to have a business. She started it because she had an experience, gained a lot of knowledge by going through what she went through, and then wanted to share that expertise and help others. She told me she didn't set out to spend her days running a business, but now she loves what she does (writing and coaching about a gluten free lifestyle, but also making a lot of unanticipated money).

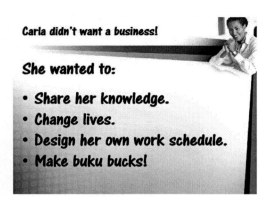

Carla didn't want a business!

She wanted to:
- **Share her knowledge.**
- **Change lives.**
- **Design her own work schedule.**
- **Make buku bucks!**

Carla had excellent knowledge of her product, but the problem was, Carla didn't have the tools or skills to get many sales. Having the skill to enroll people into her classes, courses and programs would also help Carla gain much needed confidence.

She thought of sales as slick and rude!

Never pressure people to push them into purchasing. Instead, PREVENT them from procrastinating by guiding them to make the move they likely already want to take.

Learning to generate leads and attract clients is a business skill that brings in interested prospects. Compassionately closing sales is challenging to most entrepreneurs, but learnable. You may initially meet leads from collaborating with others, networking meetings, and referrals. I have a free resource for you of other unique ways to find clients at ClaimClients.com. You want to help so many people, but how do you get them to see what you see? It's NOT about what you tell them. If you want them to buy, it's about what you ask them.

You can get in front of a large number of eager prospects who are looking for the unique services that you provide; you can network; and maybe you've even started a following, but if you haven't mastered the art of Leading A

Sales Call, then you won't get the results that you're looking for, a large number of paying clients, right? SALES BEYOND YOUR WILDEST EXPECTATIONS is about your specific prospect and their problems not about the products that YOU offer and YOUR profits.

You can convert way more Lookie Loos and Maybe Shmaybe's into Paying Clients if you understand this…It's Not About the Parts of Your Program or your process, It's About the Pain You Stop for your clients. Your prospect doesn't care as much HOW they get the results but THAT they get them! For Carla it was about the stomach cramps people were suffering from, not about the module in week 2 explaining what a wheat allergy is. Your ability to offer them the opportunity to alleviate their pain shouldn't be awkward. Closing a sale, shouldn't be awkward.

Consider what your clients are afraid of, such as, losing their home, constant stress, having their business fail. Determine what it costs your client NOT to take advantage of your offer - divorce, diabetes.
Make a list of the problems your clients have, such as "desire to lose weight," then take it further and write down how that problem might affect them in their everyday lives, such as "fitting into their clothes".

Your Offer – makes sure that you're communicating what your client desires to achieve. "Are your friends all getting married, and you're tired of getting parked at the singles table?" or "Are you tired of needing four glasses of wine just to unwind at night?" These are the problems you solve, from your client's point of view.

Have you ever met someone who already knows what you do, and they start the conversation by asking "How much do you charge?" Consider this, most people won't pay for your services until they understand the severity of their problems, the cost and consequences of not solving their problems, and the "vision" and impact of what their lives would look like if these problems were solved.

A doctor wouldn't give a prescription without a diagnosis and you shouldn't either. Asking questions in a sales conversation is not just to fact find, but to elicit whether or not your prospect finds something to be a problem. Then you look beyond the immediate problems, or symptoms, to discover their underlying issues and paint a bigger picture of possibilities for them. Let them talk about what it would be like to not have their challenge. You'll take your prospects through a path to offer them a solution for which they've been searching. Prospects find valuable benefits truly worth paying for.

So here's the antidote for "How much do you charge?" Politely respond by saying "I need to know more about what your needs are so that I can determine if I have something that will actually help you." At this point you could either ask to schedule a conversation, or you could say "I'd like to ask you a few questions first, and then I'll be more than happy to share the details of the program or product I feel would be the best fit for you or, if I know of someone else who has something that's a fit for you or, maybe I can share a free resource with you. Does that sound fair?" The timing of your offer is so important. If they don't yet have a stack of valuable benefits, they may not be ready to move forward.

The further you diagnose, the better prepared your client can be to make an assessment of their investment with you vs. continuing with the way things are now. You want to lead a sales conversation that PREVENTS objections and PREVENTS buyer procrastination.

Listening, Listening, Listening can PREVENT Objections. Sales isn't about persuading a prospect to be ready. It's about having them say in their own words what their life would be like after your service. What the change would do for them. This is how you create an Authentic Sense of Urgency. Find out their answer to "Why Now?" The insight you'll get from their answer will spark the conversation further. If you hear no signs of your prospect being ready to shift, revise, alter, adjust or make a change, I suggest you ask permission to ask more questions, and write down their responses. Having their exact words to recite back is so helpful for THEM. Take notes and use their words. They will decide themselves . . . you are there to LEAD them through the process of thinking in an organized way about the problem that they actually have. Offering before this questioning process is complete is the ultimate cause of objections.

What does your business solve in terms of problems, concerns, frustrations, worries, and challenges? Now ask the prospect if they struggle with that. Ask. Ask. Ask. Such as "Are you nervous about continuing to do X, how you've always been doing it?" Align with them. "What else is X, Y or Z effecting?"

When you improve your skill of guiding people to see the difference between the cost of their problem and the value of a solution, you'll have that sharpened skill forever. Improve your ability to draw out consequences, ramifications and implications of what will happen if they stay where they're at and you'll make more money.

The sequence to sales is step by step. Ask them insightful questions that elicit them sharing with you the payoff, reward and benefit of changing. Gain agreement on the value that THEY SAID they see in your solution. From conversation to transformation is always a partnership. This ClaimYourClients.com questioning technique and model empowers your prospects to think and evaluate for themselves in collaboration with you as their guide. For now, your job is to lead the conversation, to them deciding if they want to stay where they're at or make an important change. Then you've earned the opportunity to deliver your expertise in exchange for payment. Your resistance to selling will vanish once you've prepared and practiced your customized compassionate sales system.

I know that you're amazing at what you do (the delivery part). Whether you are a life coach, nutrition expert, or horse whisperer, you know your thing! Yet the part that we miss, time and time again, is that pesky part between attracting interested prospects and preparing for delivery of your product – Closing Sales. And isn't sales what keeps our business afloat?

Compassionate selling is about respecting the people you talk to and caring about them. Prepare your sales process by crafting useful questions. Ask the questions and carefully listen for valuable information in the answers, and respond to those answers with authentic appreciation for the transformation they desire. Ultimately, it's about figuring out if you're offering a benefit for your prospect, and believing that your offer is truly a fit for your prospect. Finally ask them "What would happen if you didn't have this problem?" The close is about the prospect acknowledging how your offer will benefit the exact issues your prospect said they're having. Be patient. Be sure they see the value of your offer. Listen and be patient.

Selling isn't persuading or convincing. It's not trickery or deception. It's helping a prospect clearly see their problems, the benefits of solving their problems and the value of your particular solution to their problem. You're giving them the opportunity to enroll themselves into your program out of their desire step forward into some kind of better self or better life… you're not pushing the details of your "stuff" at them! It's just inviting them to the next logical step.

To facilitate the "close" without feeling awkward, ask them "Are you ready to invest in yourself?" This isn't about buying something from you. You're giving prospects an opportunity.

Retaining your clients is done by delivering value (Providing Transformations, Results, Outcomes or Dreams). Knowing your expertise, is great for preventing refunds, but your initial cash flow comes from your ability to make a sale (close).

To keep your registrants excited about your program, you want to give them an immediate pre-course assignment so that they start receiving value right away. If people experience transformation before they even start the official class, they'll be talking about it with their friends, who may also be tempted to enroll.

And when they arrive for session one, they'll have more of a connection with you and your work, which may increase the likelihood that they'll want to continue working with you on a deeper level when the program is over. So have them jump right in even if your program isn't starting for a few weeks.

Enlightened women/men who can control their SALES destiny will change the world.

It's easy to share with your friends and I'd LOVE you for it. Tweet or share on Facebook: "If your business depends on sales, check out www.ClaimClients.com ."
Email Alisa@ClaimClients.com or immediately contact 908-443-1663.

Alisa Ugalde

Eric Upchurch is a Coach, Professional Speaker, Strategist, Radio Show host, Entrepreneur, and Award Winning Speaker. He has authored two administrative manuals which have become proprietary assets of the corporations they were written for.

He is the creator and author of The Life Workout Book® - a workshop in a book that puts lives back on track. He would say he is yet "a student of learning" as he leads a life of joy, completeness and fulfillment, doing what [he] was "born to do" - help others to do the same.

Eric unleashes a defined process for finding, perfecting, and presenting one's life message. He has incorporated his own "special blend" of healing modalities which draw from Neuro-Linguistic Programming, Hypnotherapy, Emotional Intelligence, EMI, Shadow Work, and what he calls Source Reflection, and incorporated them into his speaking style and training. Connect with Eric by visiting ericsupchurch.com.

There is treasure buried within the rubble of your past. Within your history are the keys others need to experience the freedom and success you've accomplished. Start today to find, perfect, and present your message to the world. To assist you in doing this, I've launched an internet based radio station which plays 24 hours per day, 7 days a week, just to get your message out to the world. Each subscription comes with a 30 minute Content Coaching session worth $175 dollars. It's yours free. See our subscription rates for pricing.

Bonus Offer: SUBSCRIBE TODAY AND YOU'LL GET 3 MONTHS ADDED FOR FREE! Go to prospeakradio.com and register today!

Chapter 15

Unearthed Treasure

by Eric Upchurch

Clutching a wrinkled piece of paper, I boldly took center stage. It seemed a long way to the front of the sanctuary, but my legs had finally carried me to where they would shake as if motorized. In the few moments of silence before I began, it seemed deafening. Without a podium, I held the microphone with one hand while attempting to unravel the paper I'd scribbled on. Struggling, I began. To say I was nervous would have been an understatement. I had only begun to muddle through my first few lines of notes to notice a number of affirming comments being periodically shouted at me from the audience. Exhilarating and frightening at the same time, the comments unnerved me, causing me to stop in my track,s if not, completely lose my place. Somewhere between a bad dream and a carnival ride, it wasn't long before it was over and I could say I had presented my first speech, at ten years of age.

This was the beginning for me. It was something about taking my seat and hearing, "Wow, you did good!" repeatedly, that really touched my young heart. It was that night that changed me forever. In words too profound to articulate, there was something about it that hooked me. I spent years studying the speaking styles of those around me. Like a sponge, I absorbed as much as I could. At seventeen, having had seven years of diligent practice and an insatiable pursuit of excellence, I strove to be the best I could. Seven years took away most of the nervousness, and instilled a calm which allowed me to stretch in other areas. At a young age, I was regarded a seventeen year old speaking prodigy, having received licenses to speak abroad.

What had at first been a comfort, soon became an annoyance. I had grown as a speaker and wasn't appeased with the now customary, "Wow, that was great!" Speaking meant more to me than hearing an accolade here or there. I wanted to change lives. Progressing beyond the mechanics of speaking, I decided to venture into what would be new territory for me.

Along with traditional schooling and courses, I absorbed everything I could get my hands on regarding Psychology, Neuro-Linguistic Programming (NLP), Hypnotherapy, and anything that would bring healing and clarity to someone's existence. My studies had taken me into territories I never thought imaginable. I saw the importance of embracing other languages, reading texts in their original tongue for added depth and meaning. Adding depth and meaning to subjects of interest meant I had more to offer those that heard me. What most fascinated me were the Hieroglyphics of Ancient Egypt which brought a fathomless depth to meaning itself.

For example, many speakers employ what I've termed a "mono-dimensional" approach to speaking: "I have what I want to say because I've got it written down right here!" While memorizing is always a benefit, many resort to drudging through their "speech" by doing little more than reading. An added vocal inflection here or there to break the vocal monotone, and they feel they've spoken worthy of applause. Certainly they have, even for just getting up and grabbing the mic.

I've discovered speaking to be so much more than an opportunity to be heard. Speaking is an opportunity to interact with an audience "multi-dimensionally". Perhaps you've heard communication is seven percent verbiage, thirty-eight percent intonation, and fifty-five percent body language. Many have sought to challenge these findings while yet being affected by the power they wield. Rest assure, even if the number crunching doesn't quite crack up to what you'd like, we become highly impressionable when these elements are strategically employed to influence, persuade, explain, introduce, or simply interact. Aside from these existing elements, there is an added element a speaker can incorporate that makes the multi-dimensional approach even more lethal. This added ingredient is an entirely different level of communication that has the power to make concepts and ideas become viral within the minds and hearts of those who experience it.

Communicating with an audience multi-dimensionally brings them into the experience of what is being said, enough to move them into action. By employing this method, I have reaped benefits which have come in many forms. My speaking career has taken me across the United States to participate in a host of events. In 2008, I received a great honor of speaking before members of the Egyptian Government. Where my feet haven't trod, I've been fortunate that my voice has. It is an honor to have been heard from Italy to South Africa, from California to England, Mexico to New Zealand, and beyond. There have been many to hear me speak and like what they've heard. I think that's wonderful, but still just another, "Wow, you did great!" The greatest joy I've entertained is when someone approaches me with only one question, "Will you be my speaking coach, will you mentor me?" I consider this to be of greater benefit than many of the other gifts I've received.

I'm thankful for every offer and believe it's due to my personal philosophy and unique method of Speaker Training. My greatest joy of late has been my participation in the World Championship of Public Speaking, as held by Toastmasters International. I was happy to compete with some of the best speakers Toastmasters and the world could offer. Belonging to one of the world's premier speaker training organizations is an honor within itself. Having earned a place in our Toastmaster District Hall of Fame, and one of the 88 best speakers in the world by Toastmasters International, is honorable as well. I feel it's an awesome accomplishment for having been a Toastmaster less than a year.

The experience of having competed was both thrilling and chilling at the same time. It's always a thrill to speak in front of large audiences, especially when speaking is your passion. It was also chilling, as you thought of your every move, word, expression, and tone, being pressed in the vise of scrutiny.

Having met and spoken to previous world champions, collaborating with others from around the world, and hearing them speak, was priceless. The journey and who I'd become in preparation for the contest, was by far the most valuable gift I'd received. Some marvel when I share of the many meetings with other speaking coaches and mentors who would spend hours at a time, tweaking nuances of the presentation. It took a great deal of time to marry the right movement and posture with the correct wording and vocal intonation to accurately express the thought intended.

Thankful for every grueling moment, I was able to take all I'd previously learned, and connect it with the more recent skills gained and help others to, "Speak To Reach." I was able to then help others make needed progress to increase sales, run meetings, persuade, convince, and interact with others. With the added ingredient mentioned earlier, I've been able to help speakers on every level; perfect, hone, and polish their speaking skills. Most of all, they now give their audiences an experience they will never forget. I'm grateful to be called upon to help others perfect their message and presentation skills.

There is something I discovered in the World Championship Contest, listening to the speakers and the messages they spoke. It was interesting to note speaking history being made. Speakers had come from all over the world to do one thing: tell their story. I heard speeches about having to take the kids to an amusement park, rowing a boat, being kids on the playground, and more. These topics within themselves, didn't appear to be spectacular at all. Yet, this was a World Championship! Surely every speech would have to be worthy of a Ted Talk, akin to rocket science, or perhaps an amazing discovery, or uncovering a conspiracy.

In fact, the winning speech's message centered on the changing of a tire! This is amazing for a number of reasons. Rather than suggesting the speech contest is of little or no value, it says the exact opposite. Let's ask, "What was gained by the winning speaker?" Well, for starters, world recognition, a hall of fame entry, and an abundance of speaking engagements with opportunities to sell their products, an immediate following of untold thousands, and yes, the title of being the World Champion. I can't think of a single insignificant item in the bunch. What does that suggest? It speaks to the importance of each of us finding and developing our own story.

It may be a story as seemingly insignificant as changing a tire, or rowing a boat. Yet, underneath the particulars, lay the very power to help and heal those in need, as other speakers have done. They took the time to note, value, and perfect their story and its telling, to help others. Many of them earn tens and even hundreds of thousands of dollars for doing simply that. Each of us have similar stories and experiences that are of value to others.

For example, when I gave my speech, "In the Director's Chair," I was honored to have both a fellow contestant and his wife approach me afterwards. His wife, nearly in tears said, "Hi, I just want to thank you, because your speech really helped me significantly! I had been dealing with some issues for years, and your speech has helped me to overcome that, I truly believe I'm out of my dark forest and headed for better things." Others have stated they'd never look at a director's chair the same again, and really appreciated my speech. The sentiment felt, and the words spoken, would have never been had I not valued my own story of being fifteen years of age.

I've learned we are much like the familiar story of the man searching for wealth. A man living in the plains of Africa was raised on a farm by his father. Their crops hardly grew and they often struggled to survive. The crops never seemed to do as well as expected because of needed clearing. The young man continued being an obedient son, fulfilling his father's wishes, clearing the land, planting crops, and continuing the struggle. A short while after the father died, the son decided to forsake his miserable and unproductive farm to find riches elsewhere. Selling the farm for as much as he could get, he resorted to traveling the country side, seeking opportunities to become rich. Having spent all he had, he heard of someone finding untold wealth in his old hometown. What he found out sickened him to the point of desiring to leave this world.

The farm he sold was poor in farming soil, but littered full of unprocessed diamonds which were the funny looking stones his father had him and his brothers clear away in order to plant.

Your diamonds lay hidden within the soil of your experiences, your history. This is why I'm passionate about helping others find, perfect, and present their message. Everyone deserves a chance to "Maximize and Monetize Their Message." Within what you deem as commonplace, ordinary, or just experiences you remember, is unearthed treasure. To find it, is to find untapped wealth for yourself and others.

Eric Upchurch

Eugene Vasconi is an author, speaker, and owner of several businesses. He has owned Communication Arts Multimedia, a multimedia production company, for over twenty years and also High Hopes Publishing which provides custom-tailored author services and full publishing of most types of non-fiction books.

Gene has written two books. "Say What: Do You Really Know What You Are Communicating?" is the culmination of his over 30 years media expertise and provides analysis and solutions to the many challenges of dealing with today's communication challenges. His second book, "For Bladder or Worse" is a humorous look at his ongoing challenge with bladder cancer. Created for the medical industry, the book gives bladder cancer patients a first-hand look at the disease, the procedures involved, and lays out a strategy for handling this potentially devastating disease by interviews with several healthcare professionals.

Gene can be contacted at (512) 868-0548 or via e-mail at mail@commartsmultimedia.com. In addition, get specific information on several websites:

- www.commartsmultimedia com --- the Communication Arts site for multimedia production
- www.highhopespublishing.com -- the site for the publishing company
- www.genevasconi,com -- the site for specific information on him and his speaking availability

Bonus Offer: Gene is offering a consultation about media production/communications, author services, or speaking opportunities as a bonus to the readers of this book. This 30-minute consultation is a $300 value and will provide you with specific answers to your questions. Please plan your questions before the call to (512) 868-0548 to schedule a time.

Chapter 16

Using Media to Change Your World

by Eugene Vasconi

In order to change the world in any way, you must first understand how the world relates to what you wish to change. Wow, that sure sounded like the beginning of a really boring college class, didn't it? Let me relieve you of this fear.

If you wish to help people understand your message, it is necessary for you to consider several things:

1. Who are the people you wish to communicate to?
2. What exactly do you intend to communicate?
3. How long a time do you have to communicate?
4. What is your method of communication going to be?
5. What is your budget or resources for your efforts?

Still sounds a bit like overkill? After all, you simply wish to make people understand you better, so all you really need to do is say something important and as clear as possible, right? Nope. Not today. Not in a world so full of television, radio, Internet, interpersonal, telephone, visual, physical, media, messages as we have. If you don't plan your communication and maximize how it will be delivered, you are probably spitting into a wind blowing toward you. It will come right back and be messy (ICK).

I lay a lot of this out in greater detail in my book, "Say What: Do You Really Know What You Are Communicating?" Yes, it is available on Amazon.com but we are going to give this a quick look in these few pages because this topic forms the basis for how you are either going to be a success in life or a failure. Yes! How you communicate affects everything you do starting at birth and ending when you take your last communicative breath.

In addition to my usual duties as a human being, I have spent most of my life engaged in the process of electronic communication; this started with several years in broadcast radio. From radio, I morphed into broadcast television and finally into all of the other blossoming forms of electronic media such as Internet development, DVD program creation, and electronic learning systems. In every case, the communication principles we stated in the beginning have guided me into making messages that have been well understood and minimally misinterpreted. So, here are your first "pearls" of wisdom:

1. Your message must be worth communicating
2. Your message must draw other people's focus

Pretty simple? Only on the surface because, in order to satisfy these two rules, you must deal with the other five items we mentioned. But, let's assume that we have something very important to say and we believe that it will be of interest to the people we will be communicating to. Let's put this to a test and see if all of this effort is worth it.

Here is our proposed message to our adolescent son:

- Son, clean your room.

That seems like a worthwhile message. So, let's analyze.

1. Who are the people you wish to communicate to?
   - Your adolescent son who is probably otherwise occupied so your message will need to be phrased tightly and in a way he will quickly grasp.
2. What exactly do you intend to communicate?
   - That his personal hygiene habits are in need of improvement and his portion of the living arrangement is below your standards.
3. How long a time do you have to communicate?
   - If he is a typical teenager, you will probably need to pry an electronic device away from his ears and communicate quickly.
4. What is your method of communication going to be?
   - Speech is a possibility but he probably responds very well to a text.
5. What is your budget or resources for your efforts?
   - Here we are not looking at money, we are looking at how much effort we wish to expend. Since there are plenty more

things to confront with an adolescent, using a lot of personal resources is not wise.

So, does this analysis change our message? I think so.

According to our criteria, your message should be revised to a text:

Son, giant people-eating bugs are infesting your room. Your mother and I are facing certain death. Please immediately discard into the trash can outside, all things not on the accompanying list. You are required to do this before you go anywhere or we will send documentation photos to your girlfriend and all of your electronics will be sold.

(Provide a list of things he can keep)

In this latest version, I believe we have addressed the requirements for an impactful message.

1. Who are the people you wish to communicate to
    a. The adolescent son and we know his likes/dislikes and made it impactful in order to get his attention. The "hook" is a requirement in all communications.
2. What exactly do you intend to communicate
    a. There was a single, pointed intent of the message … not several, diffuse items. We reinforced the urgency with the "people-eating bugs" statement.

3. How long a time do you have to communicate
    a. This was a text so it was quick and pointed. There was a time limit and penalty on the message so he could not ignore that we wished this done fast.
4. What is your method of communication going to be
    a. The text seemed appropriate to his age group. By providing this as a text, he would be able to review it and not ignore it as being a verbal comment he did not hear or forgot.
5. What is your budget or resources for your efforts
    a. We minimized our resource expenditure by using the electronic method. No breath needed to be expended.

The Times They Are A-Changing?

I have a few miles on me and so I have a perspective on the way it once was versus how it is now. In the world of media, I can honestly give you the following analysis of how to deal with using media in your communication:

"The techno-toys have changed drastically over the last 50 years but the proper communication techniques have not changed one, single bit."

Let me translate and give you an example.

Before much of today's technology was developed, the best way to effectively communicate to another person was in person, face-to-face, with honest body language, an effective message, a belief in your premise, and sincerity.

Then came the telephone in 1876; radio in 1901; television in 1925; videotape in 1951; Internet with e-mail in 1969.; first cell phone in 1973; and first text message in 1992. Wow, so many new ways to communicate and the best way now is . . . in person, face-to-face, with honest body language, an effective message, a belief in your premise, and sincerity.

Huh?

The techno-toys have overtaken us and given us tons of avenues to communicate but nothing really is different. If we can use the techniques that have always been the best ways to communicate and place them onto the new media, we win. So, our task is to learn those techniques and then learn the nuances of the electronic media to make everything work well in lieu of a face-to-face encounter.

Let's quickly take a look at the characteristics and pitfalls of the most popular electronic media. Use these tips to maximize your messages. We'll go from the worst electronic media to the least worst.

- E-mail: Is a cheap way to pass a message and is relatively universal. However, cheap can often mean unimportant. Lacks the advantage of personal contact. Also is laden with potential problems such as spam filters and mistyped addresses.

- Tip: Keep e-mails brief but heavy on the dynamics. If possible, add a graphic such as your headshot or a picture of what you are discussing. For important things, always follow up with a telephone call.
- Texting: Is a slightly better alternative to the e-mail because it tends to be more immediate. However, use of graphics is not possible and it certainly isn't a personal method even though it may seem more so due to immediacy.
  - Tip: Generic texts don't work and are irritating. Be specific to whom you text and text only for a specific reason. No shotgun texts to generate interest. Do not violate boundaries or you will be ostracized.
- Voice mail: Is an increasingly prevalent obstacle to contacting another person. Some companies have eliminated any human interaction on their phone systems; you can only get recorded prompts and almost never connect with a person. You are subjected to being filtered by someone who may not be motivated to respond especially if you are selling.
  - Tip: Don't make your pitch on the voice mail. Leave your name and number and a non-sales request. "We have a two day window to get you into a lucrative project we are building – call me immediately at …" is much more powerful than "I am selling web space on our site and think it would be good for you. Can you call me at …"
- Telephone: Is still the best electronic media form of personal communication easily available to us. However, understand that

instead of working all of the senses, you are still only working sound and not sight or touch or smell.
  - Tip: Always stand when you are on the phone and want to make a good impression. Be sure to smile – this is passed along through the sound of your inflection. Avoid speaker phones and be careful of cell phones with mediocre signal strength which slow the conversation into sounding like a two-way radio.
- Video Conferencing: Is not available to many of us but is a good way to use electronic media. The advantages are the use of sound and visual but is still lacking touch and smell.
  - Tip: Be sure of your solid technology. Nothing will destroy your message quicker than having technical issues. Most people are very limited in their technological abilities.
- Streaming video: This is essentially a television program or ad and, if created using the right techniques, can be very effective even though the touch and smell aspects are absent. The power comes from developing the video message properly and knowing the target market.
  - Tip: If you are using a video to market your business or cause, use a professional. Not doing this would be like needing a broken arm set and asking your 13 year old nephew to do it. There are many techniques and skills in play.

I hope that I have given you a little perspective on how to maximize media in your life. Use electronics to augment your message and broadcast it to many people but do not rely on it as the primary message source. You are the best message source when you look me in the eye and tell me what you think.

These techniques will help you in your quest to change the world in any way you wish. Remember, if you cannot quickly and dynamically communicate your message, the only thing you will change is *your* mind . . . not theirs.

Gene Vasconi

Makeva Walker is a Richness Expert who helps businesses and individuals establish richness in all aspects of life. She has provided "Pathways to Richness" for private clients, start-up businesses and $500 million dollar companies alike. Her advice has resulted in the acquisition of multi-million dollar profits and deals for her business clients, and in freedom, creativity and financial abundance for her personal clients.

Makeva's infectious style and in-depth knowledge provide a catalyst for her highly effective teaching. She is a sought after speaker both nationally and internationally for her wealth of knowledge and her ability to help people create lives of freedom, luxury and financial security. With Makeva, get ready for an amazing ride to greater richness in your life!

If you are ready to live a richer, fuller, expanded life that YOU absolutely love, take advantage of her special offer:

Bonus Offer: Receive a FREE exclusive coaching call, normally a $297 value, with Makeva and learn how you can:
- Feel the joy of living a purposeful life by finding balance and abundance;
- Tap into your richness and use it to enrich the world;
- Experience richness in your health and personal relationships;
- Create more flexibility in your schedule for the time to do what you love;
- Make money and help people at the same time.

As an added bonus, learn how to make money while you sleep with five strategies to *Make More & Do Less*, simply by visiting our website at *www.IAmLivingRichly.com*

Email Makeva@IAmLivingRichly.com.

Chapter 17

Make More, Do Less, and Live Richly

by Makeva Walker

I'll never forget that early autumn evening. Changing leaves circled my feet as I walked across the corporate pavilion to my car. As usual, I had to speed home, have a quick dinner and get back to work to attempt to complete the absolutely necessary tasks for the day. What didn't get done would be piled onto the next day's already impossible list and, as my to-do list grew insurmountable, my dream of a fulfilling, balanced life faded from view without me noticing.

While I was able to distract myself most days with thoughts of, "Well, I make great money," "I'm successful," "It's not so bad," or "Look at what I've accomplished," this day was different. It started when I attempted to console myself thinking, "It's okay Makeva, all you have to do is make it to retirement. Then you can be free, have fun and live the life you want."

This might have been acceptable if retirement was just around the corner. But I was only 27 years old and I had already resigned myself to leading a life so far from my vision.

Have you ever had a moment of awakening where you realized how far you had strayed from your dreams? This was my moment of awakening. My own words shook me to my core, as I realized the truly depraved state that I was in; trading financial riches in exchange for a truly rich life.

I was basing the richness of my life primarily on money! I had money, power, and material goods like a nice home and car – things that many people crave. But was I really rich? Sure, I lived in one of the richest countries in the world, and by economic standards, I was in the top 5% of household incomes in America. Sure, I had loving parents, friends, and good health. But was I really enjoying them? Was I truly experiencing the richness of life that I knew, deep down inside, was possible?

At that moment, I decided to change my life. I made it my quest to Live Richly every day, in every area of my life, especially my business. You can too.

Your career can be one of the most fulfilling, exciting, creative ways to change your life and the lives of those around you. Just think how Steve Jobs, the Wright brothers, Oprah Winfrey, Walt Disney, Mahatma Gandhi & Nelson Mandela have changed our world. And yes, I did include Gandhi and Mandela; they incited massive transformation through their work.

Your "business" can be either for profit or not-for-profit, and can be your own or that of a larger organization. It really doesn't matter what your business is as long as it is true to you (and as long as it is legal, moral and ethical, of course)!

What I have learned is that business is not merely what we do to "make a living" while trying to enjoy our real lives when we are off from work. Our work and our business are actually the way in which we can enjoy our lives and bring change to ourselves and our world.

Now, you might be saying, "not where I work, you don't know my job," or "I'm in business to make money, not to change the world," or even, "That all sounds great but I don't have the time to do anything more. I'm just trying to keep up in my business and in my life." Well, my friend, I'm happy to tell you that you can have it all, no matter your current position – and you can start right now!

There are seven powerful ways you can Make More, Do Less, and Live Richly, not only for yourself but for those around you. These tips show you how to transform your career in order to change your world:

1. Be in Love with your business. Do something you love, or that at least has aspects of things that you love doing. When you love what you do, you do it faster, better, happier and your love for it is infectious to those you come in contact with.

   If you had all the money in the world, what would you do with it? How would you spend your time? With whom would you associate? The answers to these questions will help you get in touch with work you truly love.

2. Be Passionate. I remember when I once felt like I was "checking myself in at the door" when I came to work. "Creativity and color turned off? Check. Spark and passion hidden? Check. Originality conformed into the popular corporate culture? Check." And off I went to survive my day, coming back to the real me when I returned. I remember receiving evening business calls and pretending it wasn't

a disruption, all the while anxiously waiting to hang up so that I could continue enjoying my freedom until I had to return to work the next day.

The ironic thing was that I thought it was the environment that was limiting me, but it was really me limiting myself. I acted in a way I thought was "acceptable," and was miserable as a result. If I had approached my job as my true self, my environment may have come to appreciate my unique gifts.

Don't make that kind of mistake. Find your passion and let it springboard into what you do. If that means starting your own business, go for it. If not, mix your passions into what you do. Don't be afraid to show all of your true colors and talents, even in a corporate setting. In other words, express yourself through your career.

3. Be Powerful. Would you rather be the grain of sand that falls into the pond and makes a slight ripple, or a huge boulder that causes major ripples? Most of us are living too small in our businesses and in our lives. As a result, nothing changes because our actions are hardly noticeable. Don't be afraid to take risks and make big changes when you need to, whether that means asking for a raise, hiring new employees, or going after your heart's desires.
4. Be in Service. Think of others, and good will come to you. See how you can really be in service, whether it's to the people who buy from you or to your boss. Make that your mission. Don't just produce a

product or get something done. In the end, increasing your profit or salary is about increasing your service.

Create new experiences, information, insights and offers that will inform and delight. Make your customer or boss's heart beat a little faster with the thought of what you can provide. Flip the switch for the light bulb in the suspended cartoon bubble above their heads. Look for new ways to contribute to their lives. The more of a difference you can make for others, the more of a difference you can make for yourself.

5. Be Lucrative. Just because you love doing something doesn't mean you can't be paid to do it. Musicians, authors, and plenty of other professionals get paid to do things many others do in their spare time. If you have been advising your friends which stocks to invest in for free for years or are constantly hounded to act as a DJ for all the neighborhood parties, it's time to make a change. Monetize what you love to do on some level, whether by transforming your career or by offering something small on the side while maintaining your current job.

People love to ask for freebies, and sometimes it can be hard to say no. But you have to remember that asking for the compensation you deserve isn't selfish. The financial growth of your business or career allows you to grow and serve more people. As your business or career flourishes, you can be more effective in the ways you give.

6. Be Efficient. Work on your career and not in your career. All of us have aspects of business that we don't like; minimizing those aspects as much as possible allows you to focus your energy in your genius. If you are a business owner, outsource busywork to save time for more important tasks that only you can tackle. If you are working for a company, create an organized system that plays on your strengths and reduces the hours you need to put into mundane tasks.

Much of this relies on other people. The most successful among us know how to leverage the power of networks. Associate yourself with people who can help you, whether they are outsourced employees or coworkers. Find mentors who can guide you on your journey and advise you when you get stuck. After all, if you are having a problem, chances are someone else has already found a way to conquer it. There is no need to reinvent the wheel.

7. Live in Action. Don't be intimidated by big goals. Many people don't take action on large projects because they don't know what to do first. They get nervous, thinking the goal is impossible or that they do not have the resources to make it happen.

But, as they say, Rome wasn't built in a day. Sometimes the most powerful thing to do is to take consistent daily action in the right direction. Set out a plan and stick to it, making smaller goals realities each day. Before you know it, your impossible goal will be conquered.

In the Western world, we often separate our work life from our private lives. We often think of one as laborious and the other as fun and exciting. When I was not being me completely at work there was no way that I could be happy or bring happiness to others. I knew that I was not making a difference for myself or anyone around me.

Work doesn't have to be like that. It doesn't have to be something that you do just to pay the bills. Today, as many of us spend so much time working, our work can be the most powerful agent for changing our world. Your job can be what you enjoy doing, and what you do to help others. That passion recharges you and rewards you richly. I have found money, appreciation, and growth in the right work as well as skills, leadership, perspective, relationships, and travel. In essence, our work and businesses are the best ways to change our world.

Making changes to your business, your career, or just your perspective can shift your entire outlook on life. You can make a difference for yourself and for the world, just by giving your all in the right "business" every day. So go ahead - have your moment of awakening. The grass really is greener on the other side.

Makeva Walker

Alicia White is committed to providing professional marketing design and branding strategy for your business. She knows what it takes to maintain brand consistency throughout all marketing pieces to make your first impression a lasting impression. She and her team design and print marketing literature and information products for speakers, authors, coaches, business experts and thought leaders, as well as small-to medium-sized businesses across the nation.

Serving as a Director for the Public Speakers Association and member of Toastmasters International, Alicia is well versed in helping others find their speaking voice and also enjoys public speaking. She provides rich content when speaking on "The Three Cs of Branding" and "Monetizing Your Message Through Back of the Room Products." She always motivates her audience with her captivating speech titled "Lessons Revealed through Nature" in which she shares the many ways nature acts as teacher of business practices and how we can harness the lessons of nature for our careers and/or business.

To reach Alicia for your graphic design needs, business consultation, or to book her as speaker for your event, please email Alicia@BORProduct.com or call 214-556-4947. You may also connect with Alicia at www.LinkedIn.com/in/AliciaWhite911 or at www.Facebook.com/SpeakersBriefcase.

Bonus Offer: If you are ready to start public speaking, visit http://backoftheroomproductions.com/offers/imbooked.html and sign up to receive the "I'm Booked! Checklist™" for FREE. The "I'm Booked! Checklist™" provides the essential items event planners need to adequately promote you and your speech. Once you compile your I'm Booked Kit™, there will be no scrambling at the last minute and your message will be promoted exactly how you want without worry!

Chapter 18

Fall In Love with Public Speaking

by Alicia White

I will never forget the day I discovered that I love public speaking.

I was standing in front of a group of people I had never met in a city and state that I had never visited. This was my very first time to speak on a professional level. I was a bit apprehensive and questioned if people would find value in the information I was about to share. I feared I would stumble and not make any sense, though I had rehearsed my speech repeatedly.

After I was introduced, sure enough, the words stumbled out of my mouth. I said an "um" or two, my eyes darted around the room but I continued on. After a few moments, I slowed down the pace of my speech, stood tall and made eye contact to the receptive audience. I finally felt comfortable and my words began to make sense as I had intended.

But that's not when I discovered that I love public speaking. It happened about seven minutes into the speech when I told the group, "There are the three things you must do for branding." No sooner had the words left my mouth that everyone in the audience picked up their pen, leaned in towards me, and readied themselves to take notes.

WOW! I was utterly stunned. Not only were they willing to hear what I had to say, they wrote down the information I shared! It was at that very moment that my worry and anxiety about whether or not I could provide value to a room full of people vanished completely.

Since then, I have given speeches without that concern or worry. I fully believe I have value to offer and people find my experience and knowledge beneficial to their business or personal life. Of course, I wasn't always this confident. It took a lot of time and support from friends and business associates to bring me to this realization.

Graphic design is my passion. After working in the corporate world as a graphic designer and branding coordinator, I started my own graphic design firm. It wasn't long before I had clients requesting brochures, business cards, annual reports, and billboards. Anything that could be printed or put on the web, I designed and my clients loved it!

I felt secure and comfortable being behind the scenes. I didn't need the spotlight to enjoy my job; I thoroughly enjoyed designing marketing materials and developing branding strategy to help businesses and individuals shine. Then it happened. The economy tanked and marketing budgets were slashed.

Eventually, I lost several clients. And regardless of how much effort I put into promoting my services, I could not find new clients. Instead of placing the blame on the external factors, I took it personally. I thought my skills and expertise were not good enough when that certainly was not the case. Everyone in business was suffering.

For a year, I blindly trudged along, hoping business would pick up. Fortunately, I had friends who saw in me what I had hidden away. They told me over and over again how fantastic my work was. They told others about my knowledge and expertise. They encouraged me to do things I had never done before. I had buried my worth so deep, that it took some jolting, and some well-intentioned yelling in my face, to push me past my comfort level.

And I did it. I got out from behind the curtain and actively sought the center stage.

Now, I didn't start public speaking immediately. That came a year later. First, I developed my message by deciding what services I could provide and how it would benefit my clients. I am a talented graphic designer with the ability to take someone's ideas or message and professionally design a stellar marketing piece. I have corporate branding expertise and a thorough knowledge of branding guidelines. I understand printing practices and ensure all design files meet industry standard and pass quality checks.

Next, I defined my target audience. In 2011, I decided to create a niche that had not been previously served on a grand scale - speaker branding. So I tossed out the theory that everyone needs my services, because that simply is not true, and developed my criteria for my new niche. I envisioned my ideal client as a professional woman or man between the ages of 38 and 55, who has been publically speaking for about one year and wants to speak more on a larger scale.

Because of a clear message and defined target audience, my business operations and marketing strategies are aligned to achieve business success. And with my new found love of public speaking, I can reach more people. It is my hope that you find YOUR value, recognize it fully and completely, and share it with the world!

GETTING STARTED

A lot of preparation is needed to write a speech and get on stage; and even more work is needed to generate revenue from speaking. The following exercises offer a good start.

Establish Your Message

When establishing your business message, one of the fastest ways to do so is to define a problem that your customers have.

List the most common problem your customers complain about.

PROBLEM:
_____

Next, provide a solution for the problem. The solution should be a service or product that you offer and are confident it will solve their problem.

SOLUTION:

_____

Now, take the problem and solution to formulate a message. Here is a start:
Today, many people are faced with _____ (fill in the blank THE PROBLEM).
The good news is, I can help by _____ (fill in the blank THE SOLUTION).

Rewrite these sentences so that it flows with your style providing a solution that you are proud to offer. Repeat this exercise for a few more customer problems and have them ready when asked or networking.

Define the Perfect Client
It is a common mistake to say EVERYONE can be your client. Truly define your target audience: what do they look like? How much money do they make? Are they consumers or business owners? What age range are they?

List all of the characteristics that your perfect client should have:

_____

Out of the list, choose three characteristics to narrow down your target audience. Think about the clients who you really enjoy serving or who will do repeat business with you.
1.   2.   3.

With these criteria, you can create effective marketing to people who truly need your business. Without this, you could be wasting time and money connecting with people who do not need or want your product or service.

Let's further the message you wrote in the earlier exercise by adding, who you serve:

Today, many people are faced with _____ (fill in the blank THE PROBLEM).
The good news is, I can help by _____ (fill in the blank THE SOLUTION).
_____ and_____ (fill in the blank with one or two of your perfect client characteristics) find that my services save them from _____ (fill in the blank THE PROBLEM).

Use my message as an example:
Today, many event planners will not fill a speaker role with <u>someone who does not have a speaker sheet</u>.
The good news is, I can help by <u>creating a professionally designed speaker sheet</u>.
<u>Speakers who don't have a speaker sheet or may need an updated speaker sheet</u> find that my services save them from <u>having to say no to event planners because now they have a professional speaker sheet that they are proud to deliver</u>.

Developing Your Speech

Once you have established your message, you have an idea of what to speak about. In a speech, you will share valuable content that encourages a listener to take action for a better life or business. There are three requirements for a good speech delivery. Be patient as you write.

Introduction: Believe it or not, the last exercise you completed is the perfect beginnings of your speech. Tweak what you wrote to introduce what you will share with your audience. This is a perfect time to share a case study or personal story that supports your message. Make it compelling and memorable.

Body: This part can be a little tough for some. Give real value when speaking without giving too much detail. After all, you want them to hire you to solve their problem.

Here are some ideas to developing the body:

- If you have authored a book or chapter, use one or all chapters as the outline for your speech.
- If you give worksheets to your clients to fill out, build your speech providing details into the how and why.
- Base your speech on one word. For each letter of the word, create a lesson. My friend Karen Bragg-Matthews, a life and career coach speaks on FEAR, she creates her lessons around each letter: F- Fantasy, E- Experience, A- Accept, R- Reality
- List lessons in threes using words that start with the same letter. One of my speeches is titled: The Three Cs of

Branding: Learn How Consistent, Concise, and Creative Branding Leads to Success
- Start with a problem and give the solution in several steps.
- Create a top seven or ten list of problems and highlight each with a solution.

Conclusion: Give the audience a summary of the speech by repeating the value that you want them to remember. Drive home the point of your message and how you can help solve the audience's problem. Give a compelling, "easy yes" offer. Avoid hard selling from the stage; instead direct them to the back of the room where they can talk to you and purchase your services or products.

Start Speaking!

There are several opportunities to start speaking. Check out local organizations such as the Rotary, Lion's Club, and Chamber of Commerce. Join an organization geared to speaking such as Public Speakers Association. Announce to friends and business associates that you are seeking speaking opportunities.

If speaking on stage is not for you right now, here are some other ways to share your message. The more you take advantage of these opportunities, the more you will hone your message and be ready for the spotlight.
- Radio Talk Show Guest
- Conference Break Out Expert
- Mastermind Guest Experts
- Teleseminar Speaker

- Webinar Interviewee

The power of your message should appear everywhere! Take the message you developed above and put it on everything, adding details to inform prospects how you help them.

- Booklets
- Brochures
- Website
- Postcards
- Posters
- Banners
- Social Media
- Video
- Audio

We all have a message and YOU have VALUE. It's time to share that value because you never know who you will help. Imagine people getting inspired and taking action to better themselves because of you. It wasn't long ago when I didn't realize my own value; now, I can't wait to share my message with others. I encourage you to take the next step and share your message through speaking. You will find it is a life changing, rewarding experience!

Alicia White

Change the World from the Front of the Room!

PublicSpeakersAssociation.com

DANNY GLOVER
AUTHOR - SPEAKER - COACH - TRAINER

Danny Glover speaks to audiences both large and small and loves them all. He has spoken at athletic coaches conventions, teacher conventions, military balls, civic groups, business conferences, leadership conferences, marriage conferences, and church groups.

Danny is available for keynotes, conferences, emcee, and workshops. He exists to encourage, empower, and equip individuals and organizations to maximize their potential. Danny brings a down-home humor and insightful teaching of life principles together in fun, informative, and practical speeches focused on personal growth, relationships, and leadership.

BOOK DANNY FOR YOUR EVENT:
877-256-1264
DannyG@gloverconsults.com

MOST POPULAR TOPICS:

BE A DIFFERENCE MAKER!
Do you want to make a difference? Danny shares about some of the difference makers in his life, and teaches 3 abilities needed and 3 ways you can make a difference with others.

MAXIMIZE YOUR POTENTIAL!
Every person has much potential greatness in them, and few actually tap that potential. Learn how you can discover, develop, and deliver on the potential within you!

SOLVING YOUR PEOPLE PUZZLES!
If you have to deal with people, you will love this teaching. Find out why people are so different and how you can adapt to relate to them the way they need you to relate.

Tonya Hofmann

"I'd Love to help YOUR EVENT find attendees, vendors & sponsors too!"

CEO & Founder of the Public Speakers Association, Author, Radio Show Host, International Speaker

Book Tonya to Speak at your next Event: www.TonyaHofmann.com

Are YOU READY for a website that works for you...

Most websites have 1 Personality

*Don't miss the Opportunity To Talk to:
Go Getters,
Social Butterflies,
Caregivers & Analyticals*

We've figured it all out for you!

Marketing Finally Done Simple & Effective!

Contact Michael Hofmann for a Free Marketing Analysis!
michael@StandOutInYourBusiness.com

High Hopes Publishing

Complete Author Services . . .

- ⇨ Concept Development
- ⇨ Cover Art
- ⇨ ISBN / Copyright
- ⇨ Layout
- ⇨ Editing
- ⇨ Proofing
- ⇨ Printing
- ⇨ Audio/Video support

Total package creation in printed or electronic format

1-888-742-0074
(512) 868-0548
www.highhopespublishing.com